Temptation

TEMPTATION

DIOGENES ALLEN

SEABURY CLASSICS
An imprint of Church Publishing, Incorporated
New York, New York

A catalog record for this book is available from the
Library of Congress

ISBN 1-59628-007-7

Church Publishing Incorporated
445 Fifth Avenue
New York, NY 10016

Desire, Desire, I have too dearly bought
With price of mangled mind, thy worthless ware.
—Sir Philip Sidney

CONTENTS

ACKNOWLEDGMENTS

Although a great deal in this book does not depend directly on the works of Iris Murdoch, Simone Weil, and Gabriel Marcel, it could not have been written without them. I acknowledge that at the outset, not only to avoid cluttering up the book with footnotes, but because mere notes would misrepresent the debt. What I owe them is not primarily various ideas that I have used, but having been so formed by them that their influence is never absent. Large parts of this book were initially delivered as sermons or lectures at the Princeton Baptist Church at Penns Neck, Princeton, New Jersey; Westminster Presbyterian Church, Trenton, New Jersey; and Twelve Corners Presbyterian Church, Rochester, New York. The comments of these congregations were often very useful.

There is more than one valid or accurate way to describe the Christian pilgrimage; this book seeks to give only one. It is also possible, by relying on other people's actual journeys, to describe it without having traveled very far oneself.

HOW *TEMPTATION* LOOKS TO ME NOW

I realize more than ever how remarkable it is that Jesus was subject to temptation. Since all of us are all too aware of temptations in our lives and know how easy it is to succumb to them, we may pass over the fact that the New Testament stresses that Jesus was subject to temptation. But this was not the case with the people who witnessed his resurrection from the dead and who were responsible for the writing of the New Testament. With his resurrection the outlook of Jesus' followers was utterly transformed. His glory was now manifest to them and they were in awe of him. Jesus was now seen to be Immanuel, God with us. As Paul, whose vision of the glorified Christ came only after Jesus' ascension, put it so succinctly, "even though we once regarded Christ from a human point of view, we regard him thus no longer" (2 Cor. 5:16b). He was now seen to be "Lord," a title hitherto reserved for God and God alone.

In retrospect it would have been easy for Jesus' earliest followers in light of the resurrection to consider Jesus' temptations as merely *apparent* temptations, not real ones, since God is not subject to temptation. This was how the Gnostics and Docetists responded to the divinity of Christ. For these theologians the incarnation of God the Son was not a true incarnation whereby God the Son became a human being. Rather, they taught that he just *looked* like a human being, but he was not a human being in any other way.

The gospel writers, however, firmly rejected such views. God had *become* a human being: in order for Jesus to pioneer a route for us to follow to the Father, he must begin from where we are, people subject to temptation. So the gospel writers stressed that Jesus faced temptations. Apparently, no one would have believed that God could undergo temptation had it not been so evident in the life and death of Jesus. There are some passages in the Old Testament that describe God as changing his mind, but in ancient Judaism they are generally understood to be metaphoric and not to be taken literally. But the coming of Jesus shows the full extent of God's love for us: God made himself subject to temptation in the person of his Son incarnate. The extent of God's love is measured, so to speak, by his humility in making himself vulnerable.

The temptations of Jesus also give me another reason to have confidence in the gospels. It would have been far easier for the gospel writers to leave out anything that indicated any weaknesses—such as being subject to temptations—than to record them, much less to stress them in the face of deeply entrenched convictions about God's overwhelmingly superior and transcendent greatness. But the gospel is paradoxical, combining as it does opposites in one person, refusing to allow the glory of the risen Lord, who is no longer seen from a human point of view only, to cancel his humanity. This includes reporting not only Jesus' temptations but also their importance for us.

Over the years experience has reinforced one of the main points I stressed in this book: we are never finished with temptations. The temptations that we have come to terms with at one time take a different form at a later time. For example, I thought I had finished with the temptation of material goods when at seventeen I responded to a call to ministry; you do not seek to become a minister in order to make money. Some years later when I had a family, my mind was so filled with the worry of how I was going to pay for all those school and college fees that it not only weighed down my spirit, but it distracted me from paying proper attention to other people. I could not thoroughly enjoy their friendship or be aware of and sympathetic to other people's needs. It certainly did not make life easier for my family. By the time I had found my way beyond this anxiety, I started to worry about saving for retirement, and now in retirement the temptation has become the question, Do I have enough money to last? The love of God that has been poured into our hearts makes us spontaneously generous, but I have learned that for many of us the core of avarice is not greed. Rather, it is the erosion of that spontaneous generosity by anxious thoughts of whether we will have enough—thoughts that lead us to hold back and even to crush the spirit of generosity.

A great example of the eroding effect of avarice is found at the opening of Jane Austen's novel *Sense and Sensibility*, in which a son promises his father that he shall use a portion of his ample inheritance to provide for his stepmother and his half-sisters. Although he is utterly sincere when he makes this solemn promise to his dying father, his resolve is progressively undermined by the persistent remarks of a greedy wife who, day by day, anxiously mentions that the great expenses and needs that they have in raising a family will hardly be covered by the inheritance. Bit by bit he reduces the amount he thinks he will be able to afford to give until, finally, he decides that the other members of the family are already sufficiently well off so as to not need any help. The son convinces himself that his father was simply filled with groundless anxiety over the need to provide more for the rest of his family. In this the son deceived himself badly, as it took the generosity of a relative to provide even shelter for them.

One of the elementary truths of the gospel that I stressed as a primary truth in this book is that we depend on God, and that this dependence should be a joyful one, since our Father is generous and well-disposed toward us. In recent years I have had to painfully learn what it means to live this way in a new and hitherto unexpected way. It came about after I learned that I had an incurable kind of leukemia and small-cell lymphoma. Although I was told that people with these particular cancers usually live for several years, it was clear that I would never be among the very old. Like other people I had to learn how to cope with this situation and, like most people, I got along more or less all right much of the time, in spite of the fatigue that goes with leukemia. The worse times are when you wake up during the night with symptoms that mean the disease is progressing. On one of those occasions when my usual ways of dealing with the rising fear had failed, including heartfelt prayers, I was driven to say, "I cannot carry this load; over to you, Jesus, it's yours." To my surprise the next thing I was aware of was waking up, not because I had been dreaming, but because I had simply fallen into a peaceful sleep until morning. I now realize that I cannot rely on my own faith or awareness of having faith, as I had been doing, but I can rely on Jesus' faith to carry me through this part of life that we call dying. It is quite a relief.

Finally, I have learned in retirement that what I have retired from is my place of years of employment, but not from life. This occurred to me recently in talking with a person who sought some help. He spent all his time in retirement playing golf, and other forms of pleasant and harmless entertainment. But his life had become no more than looking for entertainment. For him, work was over, life was all play. He came to see me because he needed a series of medical tests, and naturally was quite worried. Happily, the test results were good, but I do not think from this encounter with reality he came to the realization that life is not simply seeking entertainment. Unless he does, he will waste so much of life, in vainly seeking to create out of the legitimate pleasure of entertainment an artificial paradise or garden of Eden.

Even though we are never finished with temptations, we do make progress in the Christian life. The journey is like mounting a spiral staircase. We do not go round and round in a circle, getting nowhere, but, as on a spiral staircase, we ascend to a higher level with each step. Otherwise, it would be utterly discouraging to encounter the same temptations we have met earlier, even though they take a different form. Instead, such temptations reassure us that we are still on the right road and are making progress. A man I never met, who was a close and deep friend of a close friend of mine, shared what he had learned in going from apparent good health in the prime of life to the fact that he had only a few months to live. He said, "In the final analysis, we live and die either with resentment or with gratitude." To learn to overcome resentment and to live with gratitude for me has become like a beacon as the darkness that all of us must pass through grows nearer and nearer.

MARCH 2004

Part 1

GETTING STARTED

M any of us who have recognized Christ's call to follow him do not feel that we are in fact making much progress in the religious life. Our search for strength and encouragement amid the pressures of life is only partially successful; our desire for a more personal knowledge of God goes unsatisfied.

The same situation is faced by people who do not go to church regularly or at all, but who are increasingly convinced that there is more to life than they are able to get out of it, that there is more to life than is included in a secular outlook. But they do not know how to find a spiritual world. They do not know where the gateway is.

This book describes that gateway. It shows how we can begin to be religious. Our spiritual journey has a clear starting point, distinct markers along the way, and a destination to be reached. It is rigorous and demanding. But there is encouragement at every stage of the way. At this point, perhaps, all we need to know is that all those who truly seek will find. The attainment of our goal is not beyond our strength, talents, or intelligence.

The way we can start is to follow Jesus. It is often overlooked that Jesus *himself* made a journey, that throughout his life he himself was moving forward. This was evident to his first disciples as they literally followed him from Galilee, through village and town, until they reached Jerusalem where he was crucified. They also learned that if they were to keep up with Jesus, they had to make a *spiritual* journey, because he himself was making one: a journey which, as I have said, has a clear starting point, distinct markers along the way, and a destination to be reached.

This book describes the spiritual journey made by Jesus, and shows how we can travel along that same path ourselves. In doing so, we experience a new kind of life that he opened up. We start to receive the strength, encouragement, and understanding that comes from an intimate knowledge of God.

Our journey begins in an apparently unpromising way—with temptations. We do not usually think of temptations as a place to find help. But there are some temptations that stand at the entrance. There are some temptations that even to recognize as temptations and to feel the conflict of being pulled in two directions is to have found the gateway to a new path. In the very conflict, we find our world more wonderful and more dangerous than we ever before realized.

Jesus showed us the gateway we are to enter, if we are to begin to be religious, when he himself encountered three temptations just before he began to teach people about God. In facing these temptations, he pioneered a path for us to follow to reach fullness of life. So in the next three chapters, we will look at his three temptations one by one and see how, by facing them ourselves, we begin to be religious. Once we have got started by entering this gateway, we will then have a look at the steps between the beginning and the final goal.

But before we describe the gateway let us consider a bit more fully the very idea of a spiritual reality, which we seek and into which we are to enter. We enter a spiritual

Only if we are willing to *receive* can we be open to the reality of others and only so can a zone of mystery emerge. When we receive in a relationship of openness and trust, we turn loose of each other. We are not controlling or holding on. By restraining ourselves, because we respect another, we allow a new reality to emerge, a zone of mystery, in which we both participate and into which we both enter and receive. A spiritual reality can be found as we learn to restrain ourselves, learn to change in this very specific way, and thereby begin to recognize mysteries.

Not only are happiness, love, and people mysteries, but so too is evil. The path Christ pioneered was one in which he encountered evil and was victorious over it. To understand the path that he opened up and that he invites us to follow, we will briefly examine the mysterious character of evil.

We begin to discover its mysterious character as we realize how often we do not intentionally choose to do evil. Both evil and good have inherent properties that deceive us—we often do evil because we do not recognize it as evil and fail to do good because we do not recognize it as good. Evil often seems to glitter, and it attracts. It is not repulsive; frequently, it is fascinating. One of the names for the devil is Lucifer, based on the Latin word for light. He is portrayed in much ancient mythology as shining. This suggests that evil has the paradoxical quality of being in fact hideous yet appearing attractive. Thus it has the power to deceive us.

Good, on the other hand, often has no initial or immediate appeal. It is often overlooked or not seen. Consider, for example, in the parable of the good Samaritan the way the Levite passed by the stricken traveler. This was not merely from a hardness of heart. There is a level beneath which our pity does not automatically extend. It is not the same for everyone. But for many of us, when we are confronted with some kinds of misery, we have an immediate revulsion. We must make an effort to overcome it before we can show mercy. Jesus could touch lepers, who had to shout out that they were unclean so that people could avoid them; St. Francis kissed their sores, for he loved even those who were repulsive—he exhibited the character of his love by action that goes against all our natural fears. Think about what your own reaction is to seeing a person, for example, in a bus station, crumpled up against a wall, filthy and drunk or drugged. Often you will find, even when you feel sympathetic, that you also have a feeling of disgust. Sometimes we may feel only revulsion at the sight of broken people—those below the level of spontaneous pity. They are like Jesus on a cross.

Good also lacks attractiveness because it restricts us or imposes limits. God surely does come across to many, especially the young, and certainly at first, as one who says, "No! No! No!"; whereas evils attract us because they do not seem to impose limits on us. We are able to do something we want to do, and nothing is more attractive than getting our own way. We move forward smoothly, without a hitch, and enjoy the unfettered freedom. It is only later that we find ourselves in bondage to evil and then recognize its repulsiveness. As the writer of Hebrews puts it, "the mature. . . have their faculties trained by practice to distinguish good from evil" (5:14).

It takes time to overcome initial impressions and to pierce the disguises of evil and to see the attractiveness of good. It takes the experience of being fooled—of finding out that what we thought was to be rejected was actually good, and what we desired so passionately was destructive. Mysteries to be known must be entered into; and when we enter the realm of good and evil, we find that again and again in our lives we have been deceived. The more we learn by practice to recognize cases of deception, the more we are gripped by the question: Why is it this way?

The question seems to have no answer, but the very asking of it gives a strange illumination and understanding, as if one is entering more deeply into the matter. For we do not solve mysteries; we enter into them. The deeper we enter into them, the more illumination we get. Still greater depths are revealed to us the further we go. In contrast to this, when a problem is solved, it is over and done with. We go on to other problems. But a mystery once recognized is something we are never finished with. It is never exhausted. Instead we return to it again and again and it unfolds new levels to us. As we will see, we live in a universe permeated by a divine reality whose hem we touch when we encounter mysteries.

We have now gone quite a long way in describing the kind of reality into which we are to make our pilgrimage. We have also described the first great law of this pilgrimage, namely, that the fulfillment of life, the finding of a spiritual reality, depends on a great number of factors over which we have no control. We are dealing with a mystery, and this means learning how to give up being in charge, setting the terms, getting what we want. It means, in other words, learning how to receive. We have now to learn the second great law: in order to receive we must first learn how to renounce. We frequently think of religion as something that we can add to what we already have; but we are to learn that we first must make some renunciations to be in a condition to receive. It is for this reason that the gateway to the pilgrimage we are to make is the place of Christ's temptations. We, like Christ, must make some renunciations before we can move forward—he into a life that brought and still brings God to many people; we into the spiritual realm that his deeds opened up for us.

Temptation means being asked to renounce something that is good or at least needed. In the first temptation we are asked to renounce the goods of this world; in the second, we are asked to renounce security. We see in this how deceptive evil is, for we are not tempted into evil by things that are evil, but by things that are good or needful. The opening into the spiritual realm is blocked not by evil things, but by good ones. This is why a renunciation is required of us—to give up something of value, to give up pearls for the one pearl of great price. That is why the spiritual world, when genuinely encountered, is initially unattractive. In fact one of the tests for whether we have ever genuinely encountered very much of the divine reality is whether or not we have experienced this initial unattractiveness of its terms.

The third temptation has to do with a renunciation of ourselves. Again this is a renunciation of something that is of value; for we are indeed precious to God and all of us individually find ourselves to be of unconditional value to ourselves. But we are asked to renounce our will, which is our control over ourselves, and, as we shall see, this means that it is we ourselves who stand as the final barrier at the very entrance to the spiritual world.

one

THE TEMPTATION OF MATERIAL GOODS

There are so many difficulties in life that we seem to be engaged in a daily battle just to keep from going under. We struggle to keep on top of our job, maintain our household, take care of our children, cope with bad health, homework, and money problems. None of us is without difficulties, sometimes overwhelming ones. We are often advised to turn to religion for help, and in fact the phrase "Christ is the Answer" has even appeared on a bumper-sticker.

But genuine religion begins by revealing to us that Christ is the answer, not in the sense of lifting all our troubles from us, but in directing us to the place where the *right* battles are to be fought. He reveals to us where we should be struggling. He does not magically remove us from all strife, but shows us which specific struggles will lead us into a haven.

The situation then is not that there are those with troubles and those without them, but that there are those caught in a whirlpool, going around and around, and those making for shore. Christ is the answer in showing us the *direction* to take, the place where we are to struggle, if we are to find a way that leads to the kingdom of his Father.

We discover what we ought to struggle with by looking at what he struggled with. He did not calmly inform us of the gateway, but he himself labored and pioneered his way through the place we are to follow. All three synoptic gospels tell us that Jesus was tempted; and all three portray the temptation scene as a gateway through which he passed. Before he began his life's work of healing and teaching, he had to pass through temptation. Mark only records the fact; Luke and Matthew give the details so as to reveal which specific conflicts or temptations form the gateway. They tell us that there were three specific temptations, concerned with how he should direct his life in order to create a path to lead people into the kingdom. We will use the account given by Matthew.

> Then Jesus was led up by the Spirit into the wilderness to be tempted by the devil. And he fasted forty days and forty nights, and afterward he was hungry. And the tempter came and said to him, "If you are the Son of God, command these stones to become loaves of bread." But he answered, "It is written, 'Man shall not live by bread alone, but by every word that proceeds from the mouth of God.'"
>
> Then the devil took him to the holy city, and set him on the pinnacle of the temple, and said to him, "If you are the Son of God, throw yourself down; for it is written, 'He will give his angels charge of you,' and 'On their hands they will bear you up, lest you strike your foot against a stone.'" Jesus said to him, "Again it is written, 'You shall not tempt the Lord your God.'"
>
> Again, the devil took him to a very high mountain, and showed him all the kingdoms of the world and the glory of them; and he said to him, "All these I will give

you, if you will fall down and worship me." Then Jesus
said to him, "Begone, Satan! for it is written, 'You shall
worship the Lord your God and him only shall you
serve.'"

Then the devil left him, and behold, angels came and
ministered to him. (Matthew 4:1–11)

To discover the spiritual reality that is represented in
this temptation scene, it is not necessary to believe that
there is an individual called the devil or Satan. The main
points concerning *what* we are tempted by—material
goods, security, and glory—are in no way increased in
intensity or seriousness by believing in an individual
called Satan. Nor are they lessened as temptations by disbelief in him. To personify evil does make the scene more
dramatic, for we find interactions between personalities
more dramatic than any other kind. So the language of the
text, which speaks of Satan, will be retained because it is
more dramatic.

Let us begin our exploration by noting that the
Scripture says that "Jesus was led up by the Spirit into the
wilderness." It was the Spirit who took him to the place
where he was alone, to be exposed to the devil. It was not
his idea or desire to go into the wilderness. Nor did the
devil control him, or lead him to the place where a crucial
struggle was to occur. It was God's Spirit who took the ini-
tiative.

We see here the first great law in operation. We are not
in charge of the circumstances in which our spiritual destiny is decided; we do not set the terms or the conditions
by which we are to find God. We are dealing with a reality who is a mystery, a reality over which we have no control. Here we see that one of the conditions God sets without any say on our part is that we are exposed to evil.
Whatever its ultimate source may be, whatever our
responsibility for it may be, we presently are in the midst
of evil and the gateway to finding God is placed at a point

where we are tempted by evil. We must face up to it and renounce it, or we do not find the gateway to God.

The next thing we notice is that temptation does not usually come when we are ready for it. It does not come when we are strongest, when we are at our best. It comes when we are weak. It came to Jesus when he was hungry, very hungry. The Bible says that he fasted for forty days and forty nights.

This time span is symbolic. Moses fasted forty days and forty nights when he was on the mountain to receive the Law from God. Israel, on the way to the Promised Land, was tested forty years in the wilderness. And in the time of Noah it rained forty days and forty nights. Each of these Old Testament stories marks a major turning point, a major change in humankind's relationship to God. God gave Moses the Law, which was one of the conditions of the covenant—a binding contract—between him and Israel. The Exodus from Egypt was what made Israel a nation: before it they were not a people; after it they had their own land. The rain represented God's destruction of the past, a baptismal washing away of all evil and a new start for humankind after the Flood. Forty, then, is a symbol—a symbol for a *decisive* change about to take place. Here we see Jesus, just before the beginning of his ministry, being tempted. He must endure this trial—he must grasp who and what he is, who and what he stands for, who and what he offers to humankind, for in that struggle a new path to the Father is being created and made available for us.

So don't worry about whether a person can actually do without food for forty days or not. Forty is a symbol—an important one—to mark this event as the hinge on which a turn is made into a new future for all of us.

And yet, he did fast. There was no food, and he grew hungry. It was then that the temptations started. When he had grown weak, when he was not physically strong, when it became hard to see straight and clearly in the dazzling sun of that sun-drenched land, it was then that temptation came.

Here again we see a condition set by God. We are spiritual beings—spirits are beings who must choose their destiny. But we are spirits who are animals. Spirits whose bodies cause us to suffer, so that we are vulnerable and exposed, able to feel every twinge of our complex organism—to have our whole consciousness filled with blinding pain so that all else is shut out and all we can think is, "Take it away, take it away." We are spirits, people who must choose our destiny, with bodies that are vulnerable, registering every little irritation and craving our daily food. We did not decide that this should be our situation; this is a condition established by our Father.

Jesus was exposed to terrible hunger, his body giving him no rest. Perhaps he was looking at the smooth round stones that lay at his feet. They looked something like the smooth loaves just out of a baker's oven, and then it struck him, "Turn these stones into bread."

It was a temptation to use his powers to bring comfort to his body, to use his unique relationship to God as a magic wand to care for his earthly needs. That was a personal temptation he faced: to avoid the pains of a bodily life. More broadly, it was to avoid being subject to one of the common human conditions we face. It was a temptation to reject a condition set by God, namely, that we are to seek him as beings who must eat, who are vulnerable to starvation, as beings who are made to desire material goods and who can therefore become greedy, covetous, envious. To use his powers to provide food in a miraculous way when he was in trouble would have been to reject a condition his Father sets for us. He could hardly have pioneered a new way *for us* to the Father if he rejected one of the conditions to which we are subject in our pilgrimage. He must have a kinship with us; he must share our situation, if he is to lead us from where we are to the Father. As Hebrews

2:18 puts it, "For because he himself has suffered and been tempted, he is able to help those who are tempted."

But it was also for him a temptation that concerned the welfare of others. He could have made his mission to the world an attempt to satisfy people's bodily needs. He could have tried to see to it that everyone had food, clothing, and shelter; to see that everyone's sensuous needs and desires were fully satisfied.

His Father faced that decision when he made the universe; he could have protected us from all shortages, from being vulnerable to starvation. But clearly we are vulnerable and we are not fully protected. Whatever the reason for this situation, it is where we are. The decision the Father made at creation, to allow this, was now faced by Jesus. He had to ratify or to reject his Father's decision by deciding what his mission was to be—bread or obedience to his Father's will.

That was for him a temptation, a terrible temptation. For are not we all, as he was, frequently moved by compassion at the suffering of people, their terrible suffering? All people are not being fed. At the same time do not we all know that people do not live by bread alone? None of us is hungry. We have foods for our breakfast that even a king couldn't have had five hundred years ago. Orange juice, for example, was not available to lands of the north, far from the warmth of Spain or Africa. We drive cars that have more power than an entire factory had in the eighteenth century. And yet are we happy? The human capacity for unhappiness is so enormous that the entire world cannot fill it.

In the legend, Faust was also tempted by the devil, and he gave in. He was able to taste and savor all things, to have every delightful experience and enchantment imaginable. All the sweetness the earth could offer. He became bored. It could not satisfy him; it could not fill him except for a little while. There is about us an indefinable craving, an indefinable chasm that the whole world cannot fill. It may take a person a long time to find that out; for we are also animals and take animal delight in what we consume. And we should, for it is needed and it is good. But that is precisely the temptation: our need and its goodness. We consume and consume and consume, and we learn the hard way—if we learn at all—that we cannot be satisfied this way. We need it; it is good; yet it does not fill us. We find here that we are tempted into evil, not by something that is evil, but by something that is good.

So we are faced each day with the terrible temptation, the powerful pull of two forces: our need and enjoyment of goods that are of this world, and our need for the good that is not. We need *both*. For we cannot live by bread alone; we do not live without it either. How can we face that temptation?

Jesus faced it by quoting the Old Testament: "Man shall not live by bread alone, but by every word that proceeds from the mouth of God." We shall live by listening to all that God tells us. So attend to that craving in yourself that only God's words can fill. The danger is that we shall not notice or we shall forget that the world cannot satisfy us. We overlook that craving that goods do not satisfy. That emptiness is only *one* desire among a multitude of desires, and so it may easily be thought to be insignificant.

But do you remember the experience of thinking that if only I had—a what? Whatever it was, you fill it in. And remember when you got it? How wonderful it was? Remember how after a while it didn't matter so much and you wanted other things? Such experiences are of vital importance. They tell us about our restless heart, our craving. For we are tempted to forget the one thing that points us to God: our restlessness with all that the world has to offer. Only he can fill that void.

We must, in other words, forsake the world. This is what we must *renounce* before we can enter the gateway of a new reality and *receive*. To forsake is not to hate the world, or to reject it. It is not to turn from material goods—food, drink, clothing—and become an ascetic; for as Jesus said, "your heavenly Father knows that you need them all." It is instead to recognize that all this world's goods are not able to satisfy us.

In facing this temptation that forms the gateway into a new reality, we are not choosing God. To believe in God at this stage is not a decision we can make: for God is initially unimaginable to us, and until we enter the gateway, we do not have a proper idea of the kind of reality God is so that we could choose him. All we can do at this stage is to decide not to give ourselves to anything that is of this world, to anything that we know or can imagine. It is not to allow a thirst and a hunger for what the world cannot satisfy to be blunted by gluttony, or smothered by greed for possessions; or to let our lives become filled with covetous desires for goods, or to seek to establish our personal importance and worth by our homes, our cars, our style of life. It is not to have our consciousness saturated by envy for what others have and what they have achieved. It is not to become callous to the needs of others and fail to share our possessions.

All this sounds negative, but to withhold ourselves is to allow ourselves to be open to a new reality. All of these desires stand as barriers at the gateway, and any one of them can keep us from entering. For they can be what we keep turning our attention to, so that the single, bare, unique desire that cannot be satisfied this way is lost to view. We must hold to it with such attentiveness that we thirst and hunger, yearn and long, for what we cannot even imagine. This is what it is to seek for the kingdom first and not to have our whole attention filled by what we shall eat, drink, wear, and possess. For though it is but one item among the many that make us up, it is not a small insignificant desire; instead it is vast because the whole world cannot satisfy it.

But suppose we are not gluttonous; not consumed with a sensuous passion for food or possessions; not seeking status through money. Suppose we do not envy others but are quite content and even grateful to have what we have; not callous toward the poverty of others. We might be quite free of all these, and yet still not find the gateway. We may miss the gateway because we are so conscious of human suffering. We may be so upset by poverty and our mind so filled with human misery that we fail to notice the small craving we and others have for what the whole world cannot give. It gets pushed aside. But Jesus retained that craving, and never lost sight of it as he faced the hard fact of human hunger. We saw *both* sides: the terrible suffering of people who lacked bread, *and* the fact that we do not live by bread alone. He did not reject or ignore the second half because of the first. The strain of keeping aware of both is terrible, but it is a strain that is unavoidable, if we are to find God. We can fail even to see that there is a second half because we attend only to the more obvious need people have for bodily sustenance. We fail to find the gateway because we fail to face the tension between human need for material goods and the need for what this world cannot supply. It is at the point of tension that we find the gateway. Avoid the tension by saying that both a world of suffering and a loving Father simply cannot exist, and we fail to find the gateway. Only after facing the tension and entering the gateway can we learn to endure a universe with such suffering. We are never to condone it, for we are always to strive to overcome such suffering. But once we have entered the gateway, we can endure what we cannot relieve, and still trust, because we know that there is a loving Father. We can trust him even though we do not fully know why there is so much suffering. At this stage in our pilgrimage, however, all that we are asked to do is to retain that small craving that the world cannot satisfy and not allow it to be pushed aside by the horrors of poverty.

We may be deflected in still another way by our concern for others. We may be free of greed; not overwhelmed by human misery; we may share our possessions by our support of good causes—and still not find the gateway. Our problem may be that we are so conscious of material goods, so preoccupied with their value, that we do not see at first that everyone needs more than bread alone. Our whole attention is devoted to people's material needs. The genuine value of material goods may cause us to underestimate people's non-material need. To care that others have enough, even to care so passionately that we, with the best of intentions, support radical political or economic views for the systematic redistribution of wealth, may lead us to sell people short. We may fail to recognize that people need more than bread alone. Preoccupation with genuine need may keep us from attending to a need that cannot in itself be named. We often fail to see that we think only of this world.

At this stage, before we enter the gateway, we quite understandably know only this world. Even so, we long for something more. We sense that this world, however desperately we need it and however wonderful, is not all. We need and crave for something we do not understand. *What* we need we cannot yet imagine, much less know. But we can and must forsake the world in a particular way. That is, we can decide not to give ourselves to this world; we can keep at least one focus of our attention on that single desire that has no name, that longing that receives a name only after all other efforts to satisfy it are renounced. At this point we enter the gateway. And we are met in this act of renunciation by a mysterious presence. Then we know. We have felt the hunger and thirst for God.

So the first temptation we face, if we are to find the gateway into a new reality, lies in our attempts to meet our real bodily needs and desires. It is a critical moment. What we do here determines to whom and to what we belong.

Sometimes in the very name of Jesus, we use religion in order to get material goods. We all occasionally long for God to satisfy our desire for prosperity and success. We hear about popular religious movements led by people who tell us that Jesus helped make them a success. They claim you can attain your goals by prayer. Yet in the wilderness Jesus himself rejected the use of his special relationship to God to get material goods.

Jesus did tell us, as we have seen, that if we seek the kingdom first, then the food, drink, and housing that his Father recognizes we need would be obtained. He knew that his Father does not so govern the world or overrule people's actions that there is no hunger. Jesus apparently was teaching us that people who seek the kingdom will not necessarily starve *because* they seek the kingdom. They may starve for other reasons, but not because they seek the kingdom. He also instructed us in the Lord's Prayer to pray for daily bread. But that is all: *daily* bread, not for prosperity or wealth. Nowhere did Jesus, who taught us that we cannot serve both God and mammon, offer his name or his Father's as a means to prosperity and success.

The need for that which bread cannot satisfy is initially a private inward desire, but it has outward, social significance. The gospel is not bread, but it is concerned with *how* bread is earned and *how* it is distributed, because the gospel is concerned with justice. The second great commandment is that we are to love our neighbor as ourselves, which surely must include treating our neighbor with consideration and fairness, and making it our business, as the good Samaritan did, to see to it that others are treated properly. The way we do this reveals how well we love our neighbor. The inwardness of our hunger, then, should not make us think that the gospel is unconcerned with social matters.

This brings us to a new point. We who are making a pilgrimage live in a particular society and nation. Our spiritual welfare is affected by our society's way of life; for our attitudes toward wealth and our economic activities and goals are very much influenced by society. So we can gain some helpful insights by looking at the pattern of economic life this society has developed. We may gain some additional perspective by looking at ancient Israel, though it, unlike our own nation, was dedicated to God.

In the Old Testament we find that the Jews as a nation faced and at one time succumbed to temptation. When they entered the Promised Land, they found it occupied by a people who were farmers. They themselves were sheep and goat herders. They did not know the techniques of farming. So they had to learn from the people of Canaan. But these people worshiped idols, which were called "baals." They believed that these gods made the fields fertile. Without offerings to them, crops would fail. Their fertility worship was also concerned with reproduction of human beings, and involved temple prostitutes. These, as well as sacrifices to the baals, were believed necessary for the land to produce food.

So the Israelites were faced with a temptation. They did not know farming, but they did know that their God who brought them out of Egypt had told them to have no other gods. They needed to raise crops, but they also knew they should not worship the baals, which the agricultural "experts" told them was necessary. What were they to do? They had to have food, yet the means of getting it were not in keeping with their religion. They succumbed to temptation. We find worship both of God and idols, so that much of the Old Testament is full of the prophets denouncing the priests of Baal. At one time the worship of God was almost gone in Israel.

Our nation is not officially dedicated to the biblical God, as Israel was, and the populations of many nations are not even nominally Christian. Yet our nation and every industrial nation has made increasing the gross national product its primary goal. Increased production is looked upon as the necessary condition for the satisfaction of all our needs. Although the benefits of an industrial economy are great, and few want to give all of them up, heavy stress on production has serious spiritual consequences. The goal of production is crowding out that small craving for something besides goods. We are subjected to terribly effective advertising designed to make us consume far more than we need in an extravagantly wasteful way and we are encouraged to go into serious debt. The sheer volume of television, newspaper, magazine, and billboard advertising dominates our attention and tends to smother any thought that fullness of life cannot be found in all this. It feeds the powerful social pressure to be like others by making people feel that if they have any second thoughts about the wisdom of this kind of life they are "Puritans" afraid of enjoyment. This massive commercial advertising is justified on the grounds that we cannot keep people employed unless there is a very high level of consumption. So we continue to rush pell-mell to keep our economy going: ripping up the earth, filling the sky with smoke, moving people around helter-skelter, filling nearly everyone with tension and anxiety. For we all need bread, don't we? We certainly do. But how much? How much do we *need*? Can that tiny half-formed thought or uneasiness in us, that yearning for something more, or different, survive? Can it enable us to act more wisely? It seems at first sight too small a thing to be effective.

Yet the kingdom of God is compared by Jesus to a mustard seed, which at the beginning is the tiniest and most inconspicuous seed. But it produces a large plant. It is not amazing or improper that we desire material goods, for they are good. It is not surprising that we are so concerned about unemployment because it is indeed hard to organize and keep going a vast and complicated industrial society from which so many benefits are derived. There are real economic problems and dangers. But what is surprising is how arresting are the words, "Man shall not live by bread alone." Their truth penetrates deeply into us. They hit us at the center of our being. And they can be the beginning of becoming religious. You may not think of yourself as religious, you may not even be seeking to become religious, but you are pointed in the right direction if you sense within you the hunger these words articulate.

We only need to hold fast to this hunger and not be diverted from it. We only need to resist using all the goods our society so abundantly puts before us as substitute foods. If we hold to the fact that we *do* hunger and thirst for that which is presently nameless, then Jesus tells us we are blessed; for we *shall* be satisfied. We are to attend to that hunger and thirst. We are to renounce anything that would divert our attention from it. This puts us at the entrance to a path that leads to a new reality that will feed us. By our hunger, we reach a place in our lives where we recognize that we are *dependent*; we are not in charge or control. We need to be fed. We are then in a condition in which we are able to receive. That is the condition in which we must be in order to receive a mysterious reality. If we have found this entrance, then we are ready to explore the second arch to the gateway: the temptation of security.

two

THE TEMPTATION
OF SECURITY

Each time Jesus is tempted, he replies with a quotation from the Old Testament. During much of his career he relied on prayer; he often went up to the hills alone to pray. But in this case, when temptations strike, we find him relying upon the explicit teachings of Scripture.

This suggests that, when tempted, we should do the same. Perhaps we cannot always rely on our feelings to tell us what to do; for at such a time our feelings are mixed. We are being pulled in different directions. At such a time, common sense, good advice, trying to work it out on our own, may be unwise. Perhaps like sailors or astronauts—who look to the fixed stars to get their bearings—we would do well to use a point of reference outside ourselves. Jesus relied on the Scripture to guide him: the words of his Father.

Unfortunately such a resource is frequently not available to us, because the Bible is too unfamiliar. A survey showed that the majority of churchgoers could not name the four gospels. A friend of mine who taught Bible and Ethics at a private girls school once told me that at the beginning of the course he asked the girls to write down the names of as many prophets as they could think of. He used to find on the list David (because of the film *David and Bathsheba*), Samson (again because of the film), and some even put Delilah. There is indeed no virtue in memorizing the names of the books of the Bible or in being able to recite the names of the prophets. But these samples do suggest a lack of familiarity with the Scriptures in a land where nearly two out of three people are attached to a church. Often we are too poorly armed to face temptation because we lack a knowledge of the Scriptures that could give us some much needed guidance.

It is interesting that after the first temptation, when Jesus responds with a quotation from Scripture, the devil introduces the second temptation by quoting Scripture himself. Jesus uses Scripture, so the tempter uses it too— uses it skillfully to entice him into evil. This is surely a way in which we can be led into evil, or a way we can use the Bible to justify our evil—to say, "What I am doing is all right, for the Bible says it is all right." Romans 13:1, "let every person be subject to the governing authorities," was used to justify obedience to Hitler, in spite of his appalling persecutions. So it is not enough, when you need guidance, just to know some passages of the Bible and be able to quote them; Satan knows that isn't enough. He quoted it to tempt Jesus into evil. We too can be misled by Scripture used as a cover to justify evil. We must know the Bible well enough to avoid such a misuse. Jesus did. To the second temptation, which the devil sugared with verses of Scripture, Jesus replied by quoting *another* passage of Scripture that showed how we were to interpret the Bible. Let us follow that discussion and see in detail the way he and we can be tempted by apparently sound religious teaching.

In the second temptation, the devil takes Jesus to Jerusalem and sets him on the pinnacle of the Temple (perhaps by means of a vision). He is then told to jump. If you are the Son of God, you will be protected by God's angels. They will catch you before you dash yourself to pieces.

Why is that a temptation? One possibility is that there is an element of self-doubt in Jesus. Is he really sent from God? Just before being driven into the wilderness, he was baptized by John the Baptist. Matthew writes that on that occasion a dove-like thing descended on him—symbolic of the Spirit of God—and a voice was heard saying, "This is my beloved Son." Matthew's description is highly symbolic. But even if we take it as an actual dove and voice, it is still possible to believe that Jesus later had doubts in the wilderness. Looking back, Jesus might think that those baptismal events were merely a hallucination—the products of crowds and overexcitement. In the wilderness the strong sense of assurance he felt at his baptism might have begun to ebb. If so, then the power of the temptation is evident. In his search for reassurance, in his attempt to regain his confidence, he would be tempted to test God and put all doubt to rest. The method is put before him: if you are the Son of God, you ought to be able to jump from the Temple. After all, the Bible says that God will protect you from harm. So here is a way to set all doubt to rest— jump from the Temple, and if you are rescued then there is no more doubt about who you are.

Such a way to find assurance seems perfectly permissible, because of the passages of Scripture, "He will give his angels charge of you," and "On their hands they will bear you up, lest you strike your foot against a stone."

Imagine the kind of dialogue that would then take place. "Go on! What are you afraid of? You are the Son of God, aren't you?" (Yes.) "Are you sure?" (Yes.) "Really sure?" (Silence.) "Absolutely sure?" (Yes.) "Well then, why not jump?" (Silence.) "Are you sure you are not afraid?" (Yes.) "Yet you won't jump. How interesting!...Look, I'll put it to you straight. Do you firmly trust your Father?" (Yes.) "All right, then prove it. Jump! Go on, jump!"

Maybe this is what happened: a surge of self-doubt and a longing to overcome it, a longing to have some surefire display that he was indeed the Son of God. But if it was, this was not all that was involved. Yes, Satan did approach Jesus as though attempting to sow doubt. But there was something else concealed in his approach. Let us try to uncover it. Concealed in this attempt to sow doubt there is a temptation over the *kind* of life Jesus was to lead, the *kind* of message he was to bring. When Satan says, "If you are the Son of God, then do this or do that," he implies that such acts are what a Son of God would do. He speaks as if turning stones into bread and jumping from the Temple are the kinds of things a Son of God would do. He doesn't argue that they are; he just speaks as if it were a matter of course that this would be Jesus' behavior. His frontal attack is to sow doubt, or at least to try to. But concealed in that more obvious attempt is the subtle, casual presumption of what the Son's behavior would be—as if this were not a matter at issue between the two of them at all.

But in response to this presumption, Jesus in effect replies, "Precisely because I am the Son, I will *not* do these things." Such deeds would be contrary to the very essence of his sonship. Instead of proving that he was the Son, to do them would prove that he was not!

This is what we discovered with the first temptation. As we saw, to have turned stones into bread would have removed him from the vulnerability to starvation that all people face. He could have tried to make himself immune from that threat by making use of his special relationship to God. He would then not have shared with us one of the conditions under which we make our spiritual pilgrimage. He then could not himself have blazed a trail for us to follow to the Father, since he would not have started from where we are. Precisely because he is the Son, he will not turn stones into bread. Precisely because he is the Son, he will not use his special relation, his special powers, to avoid being where we are—vulnerable to starvation. He hazards starvation. He trusts in his Father's care, as he seeks to open the kingdom for us to enter.

Let us now explore the second temptation and see if there are not good reasons why he will not jump from the Temple, not because he doubts his sonship, but precisely *because* of his sonship. Let us explore it as a temptation that concerns the kind of life he is to lead, that is, the kind of Messiah or Christ he is to be. In other words, What is it to be the Son of God, seeking to lead us to the Father?

Jesus was faced with the task of convincing other people who he was. He had to do something or give us something that we can recognize as coming from God. There was a tradition that the Messiah when he came would appear on a pinnacle of the Temple. Had Jesus chosen to make such an appearance, it might have had the character of a "sign." When the New Testament speaks of "signs," it often means deeds that reveal God to people who have spiritual discernment. Without spiritual discernment, the significance cannot be recognized and understood. So an appearance on the pinnacle of the Temple, if performed as a "sign," might have been a perfectly permissible act. It would have been a way of making the claim that he was the Messiah, a symbolic way of saying, "I am the Christ." In itself, it would prove nothing. It would still take spiritual discernment to recognize in the rest of his deeds and teachings that he was indeed the Christ.

But the temptation is not merely to appear on the pinnacle. It is to jump from it with the expectation that he would be miraculously saved. Such an act would not be a sign requiring spiritual insight to be understood. It would be a way to prove to anyone who saw it that he was the Messiah. In addition, it would satisfy a very common expectation concerning what God does for us, namely, protect us from danger. Jesus could display his special relation to the Father by a spectacular act of divine protection. By jumping and being miraculously saved, Jesus could then have said, "Follow me, for God's special care is on me; I have jumped from the Temple and been protected. I will see to it that protection is extended to you as well." He would overcome the difficulty of convincing people who he was by a miraculous display in which something that they expected God to give to people—namely, miraculous protection—had indeed been conferred.

There is a very strong connection in our minds as well as among the people in Jesus' time between faith in God and being protected from harm. Faith in God's goodness and love, indeed, faith in God's very existence, is deeply bound up with the idea of his care. We certainly are upset when we see a good person, who has been a wonderful neighbor and a fine parent, suddenly struck down by a terrible disease or accident. How can we believe in God, a loving Father, then?

God when he made the world faced this problem: he had to decide whether there were to be creatures who were not only spirits—that is, able to choose their destiny—but also spiritual animals, creatures liable to harm and destruction. And moreover, given that there were to be spiritual animals liable to injury, he had to choose whether he would intervene and suspend both nature's destructiveness and the harmful effects of freely chosen evil. We know the choice he made: he decided that our situation would be one in which we would have to find him, learn to trust him and love him, while we are exposed to injury and destruction.

This choice that the Father made now came to Jesus as a temptation. Jesus had great compassion for those who suffer, and he was faced with the temptation of asking that the Father protect us from all harm; perhaps even to demand that he protect us. And why not? Doesn't God love us? Isn't he master of heaven and earth? Doesn't he know when even a sparrow falls? Then why not expect such care? Why not look to him to show his love and care and concern for us? Otherwise how can we trust him? How can we believe or have faith in him?

Once again we discover that we are not tempted by something that is in itself evil, but by something that is good. For we are fragile. We can easily be hurt and even destroyed. A slip off a ladder while doing simple home maintenance; a momentary lapse of attention while driving; a virus or an unexpected strain on the heart, and our life is gone. People we dearly love, whose lives are so intertwined with ours that we cannot distinguish between their welfare and our own, can in a moment be seriously injured or utterly destroyed. Quite naturally we seek whatever protection and security we can find. We constantly try for better safety measures on our highways, protection in our factories and mines, and advances in medical knowledge. All of us go as far as we can to protect ourselves and those we love. We know, of course, that our own power and knowledge are limited. Yet we long to be completely safe, to have an assurance and a confidence that we and those we care for are safe.

It is at this point, the point where our technology reaches its limit, where our safety cannot be guaranteed by any human means, that we are tempted to call on God. We know that prayers are offered for the sick—so apparently some people believe God can help cure or relieve illnesses. We have heard of and perhaps even know people who have turned to God in extreme danger and asked to be delivered. And we sometimes hear those who survive ordeals claim that though others perished they themselves made it because they trusted in God. Is this bad? Is it wrong to turn to God for help and protection?

We have been taught by secular thought that it is. It has been argued that religion has declined in western culture because of our increasing knowledge of the natural world and the human body. Prior to the rise of modern science, people did not understand nature and disease very well. With medical knowledge and technology so limited, it was natural to look to religion for assistance. But this reliance on religion, claim the secularists, was unfortunate. It turned people's attention away from a study of the natural world and hindered the growth of knowledge that could offer effective protection. Today religion is not a serious obstacle to the advance of knowledge, but it is claimed that it retards the development of personal maturity. It encourages us to think that we can make ourselves fully secure by appealing to God for protection whenever our scientific means reach their limit. But really we cannot ever make ourselves fully secure. To suppose we can is to indulge in wishful thinking; to call on God for help reflects an incapacity to face our inevitable and ultimate vulnerability. True maturity is to face the fact that there is no complete security.

This secular view contains a grain of truth. It reflects in a distorted way a truth of Scripture: some human misery is inevitable. We cannot avoid every encounter with disease and accident. Dangers are unavoidable. The secular view endorses without realizing it the Scriptural truth: rain falls on the just and the unjust alike. However, in rejecting the idea that God will protect us, the secularists are actually rejecting only a false, misguided religion. This misguided religion, just like its secular opponent, assumes that God is *supposed* to give special protection to those who call on him. The two views merely disagree over whether he in fact does or does not protect us. Both views ignore the Scriptural text that rain falls on the just and unjust alike.

We can see something of the falsity of their assumption, as far as Scriptural religion is concerned, by the way Israel once succumbed to the second temptation. Israel thought that Jerusalem could never be conquered because the Temple of God was there. Israel assumed that because it had a special relationship with God it would be saved from its enemies in its various wars. Otherwise God could not carry out his purposes. And indeed, there were times when, though destruction seemed imminent, the city was spared. But eventually it was captured and the Temple itself destroyed. They learned that their special relation to God did not give them special immunity.

We may see more deeply into the reason why we lack an immunity from all harm by exploring why Jesus did not ask his Father to give us such protection. He rejected the second temptation because of another great spiritual law—the third we have encountered—namely, that from suffering can come understanding.

Great care must be exercised here. This law does not mean we are to *seek* to suffer; nor does it mean that there is any goodness in suffering as such. Although we are able to avoid and alleviate suffering, we cannot remove all of it. There is suffering that is beyond our control. We can do nothing about the past. We cannot relieve the suffering now taking place without such a lapse of time that much of it has taken its toll before our aid can reach its victims. As for the future, there is little evidence to think that Utopia can be attained by our efforts. Some suffering is inevitable. But, from the fact of its inevitability and from our own personal suffering as well, we may learn a great deal. One thing we can learn is that we are animals, sub-ject to the natural workings of the universe just like all other creatures from atomic particles to stars. This truth is not a theoretical matter, but in the pain we feel, and in the compassion we have for others. We discover what it means to be limited. Our limitations become a truth that is pressed into our very flesh. We learn what it means to lack complete control over our lives.

We are tempted to avoid learning this truth. We do not like to let our minds linger on the inevitability of human suffering. It causes many of us genuine distress. And when we ourselves, or those we love, are in pain we naturally look for relief. This is perfectly all right. But if we call upon God to relieve us, to intervene on our behalf just as unconditionally as we call upon drugs and machines to do our will, then God becomes part of our technology. We would be masters, in control of the situation, even though we call upon God. We would be able to escape from the limitations within which all other creatures must operate. We would thereby never experience and feel the fact that we are animals, subject like all creatures to wear and tear, and accidents. We would be living in a fantasy world, if, whenever we happened to feel threatened, events were not allowed to follow their natural course simply because we made an appeal to God. Others might fall, but not us. We would have a magic wand that enabled us to control the world for our personal safety. We could never learn or experience the fact that we are not in charge of our lives.

We encounter a mystery whenever something limits us, something that is not removable but stands as a necessity. A few examples of these mysteries might include such situations as unrequited love and our choosing of evil. Here we encounter another: that we who are indeed loved by God are nevertheless not protected from injury and misery. We can avoid looking at destructiveness. But injury and misery are there whether we pay attention to them or not; they are real whether we distort them in the name of religion by piously calling upon God to deliver us from all harm; they are not removed from the world.

But in facing human misery and pain openly, we may be given a special opportunity to learn from suffering. The inevitability of human misery despite all our efforts can help us start to discover ourselves, to discover what we are and where we are. If everything gives way to our desires, to our wills, then the entire world is subject to us. It becomes our world, our possession, by being subject to our will—even though we must use God as a means to effect our will. It takes something that resists us, that does not give way, to act as a landmark for us to find our place. Dangers, illness, accidents, disease, decay, and death are not in the last analysis problems for which there are solutions. Although most of them can be and rightly are mitigated, there is no way to remove them totally from human beings as a species. There is no way to avoid being liable to them personally.

They are mysteries, ones that can help get us into a condition to find a spiritual reality. But their value as mysteries can be concealed from us. False boasts of the power of human technology or complete reliance on human achievements can veil the inevitability of some human suffering. Reliance on false religious claims that promise us that we personally can escape dangers and suffering can close us off from an encounter with the reality of God. Sometimes the only way these concealments can be taken away from our sight is for us personally to suffer or for those we love to suffer. Sometimes it seems to be the only way we are brought face to face with what we are—creatures, liable to harm and with no sure way to avoid it. We then have the opportunity to learn that it is in this kind of world, a world with danger and no immunity from it, that we are to learn to find God, to trust God, and to recognize his love.

Without realizing it consciously, we sometimes make our security a test of God's reality or of his love. We assume without saying it even to ourselves that in some specific matter or other we expect God's protection. This may become apparent to us or to others only when we ourselves become stricken by a disease that leaves us crippled. It may come to light when a heart attack makes it questionable whether we may ever again be able to lead the kind of life we had always taken for granted. Our assumptions about God's care may come to the surface for us when we lose a child or have a miscarriage. Our faith in God is suddenly gone. We seem to have been abandoned. The world now seems completely altered: it is now cold and indifferent, when before it had seemed supportive. We may then discover that we had all along expected God to give us security. We had assumed that if there is a God, he must protect us. We discover that we had assumed all along that if God does not care enough for us or for those dear to us to protect us, then the words, "God loves us as a Father," are empty. If we aren't protected, we conclude there is no God.

It is perfectly natural to want to be secure. But we may, without realizing it until tragedy strikes, have made our security a condition for God's reality. Our security, we assume, is something he must grant, if we are to trust him. Such an unspoken but active assumption takes it for granted that we are in charge of the conditions in which God's reality is to be found. We assume that we know the conditions that he must meet, what he must do, in order for us to know that he does or does not exist. But the discovery of his reality, the discovery of the nature of his love, is not in our control. God loves us, but that does not mean he will invariably protect us. He is a mystery over which we do not possess power, which we do not begin to understand until we submit to his conditions. We must renounce our demands for personal security, our demands that there be no human misery, before we can receive assurance of his reality and love.

Jesus did not call on God to get him out of dangers. He tells us, when he is arrested, that he has power to summon legions of angels to save him. And, when he is on the cross, his enemies wait to see if God will rescue him, and they taunt him when no help comes. The assumption is that God can and does protect his own. In the garden of Gethsemane Jesus does ask his Father to deliver him from an ordeal, but then, as throughout his life, he recognizes that he cannot be immune from all danger and suffering, and in particular from the ordeal of the cross, so he adds, "Nonetheless, thy will be done." His trust in God is shown to be complete by his confidence in his Father's love even when he is undergoing suffering.

Had he demanded an immunity from harm, had he made stipulations about which losses or tragedies would show there was no loving Father, he could not have pioneered a trail for *us* to follow. He would have expected to be spared from living under the same circumstances as we do. We are exposed to danger, suffering, and loss. He resisted the temptation to use his special powers, his special relation with the Father to gain or demand immunity from such exposure. He did not try to be in charge of the circumstances in which he was to serve us. He did not try to set down the terms in which he had to work for our redemption. Instead he renounced his will, his inclinations, his desires, and accepted his Father's will. He took his place alongside of us, and made his way to the Father from where we stand. By this obedience to his Father's will, he became for us a way to the Father.

We too can discover how without realizing it we make assumptions about the circumstances in which God is to be found. We can discover those assumptions that hinder us, and by shedding them find the gateway. Each of us may be hindered in a different way. We may, for example, share the secularist assumption that the very idea of a loving Father is utterly irreconcilable with the fact that people suffer. All of us feel the force of the conflict sometimes, and we should. Clearly we ought to be disturbed by suffering. How is it compatible with God's love?—even Jesus felt this conflict. He was compassionate, and deeply moved by human suffering. He sought to relieve it again and again. Yet he recognized that from suffering can come understanding, an understanding that is not merely theoretical but personal. From it we learn what it is to be a creature and that if we are to find a loving Father, it is as a spiritual animal who is not immune from harm. We miss the gateway when we lose the opportunity to learn from suffering. The love of God is to be understood not apart from human suffering, but by openly facing suffering. We can reject God's way without realizing we have done so, by neglecting to face human suffering and to learn from it.

Our very "religiousness" may keep us from facing suffering. We may hold, without fully realizing it, the assumption that a loving Father would not let harm come to people who are devoted to him. We might not admit holding this assumption, but in practice we operate with the expectation that we will be protected from devastating loss. We may notice only that things go right for us and our circle. We do not allow the reality of famine, wars, and the torture people endure to touch us personally or deeply. We know they are there, but we keep them at a comfortable emotional distance. In effect we push them aside as somehow outside God's providence.

Others of us keep human suffering from penetrating personally by a theory about how God and evil are reconcilable. A favorite theory is that people are responsible for evil. There is a lot of truth in this theory, but we avoid learning from suffering if we think the theory explains everything. Whatever the ultimate reason for suffering and however responsible human beings are for it, it still happens. There is no escape from this reality. Misery is around us and none of us is ever free from personal threat. Only when we learn from suffering, when we learn personally what it is to be a creature, vulnerable to destruction, can we begin to find and to know what it is to have a loving Father.

Whether we like it or not, a condition that God sets is that for us to find him we must learn from suffering. It does not necessarily have to be our own; we do not *necessarily* have to suffer terrible loss ourselves. We can learn from the suffering of others, whether these others are near us or remote in space and time. We can learn that we personally have no immunity, that we have no way to guarantee our security, that we—whether we like it or not—are deeply dependent on circumstances over which we have no control. To learn this from suffering is part of the path we are to walk if we are to find God, instead of an idol made by our own imagination and subject to our wants and wishes.

Not only are we to learn for ourselves that we are limited, dependent, unable to control all things, but suffering also can teach us something else that connects the first arch of the gateway with the second. When we are told that we do not live by bread alone, when we are told to seek first the kingdom, when we are called to give up a lot of desires—I think we could do it, if... if we were *sure* that there is a kingdom. We could turn from our restless craving to possess, if we just knew for sure that there is a God. The first temptation would not be so powerful, so overwhelming, if we just knew.

But that is just what we encounter in the second temptation: the absence of security. This time it is the security of a knowledge that would enable us to overcome the lust for this world, a knowledge that would assure us that we don't have to cheat, to drive ourselves into the ground, to consume ourselves with envy of others—because we have a heavenly Father. We could know that we have such a Father by seeing his care for us; by having disease and accident and danger removed from us when we pray.

So much religion in our land is a religion of "God protects us from the ordinary dangers of life," so that "our foot will not be dashed against a stone." Sometimes it is explicit, as it was among the Jews when they expected their Temple to make Jerusalem impregnable. Sometimes it is a quietly made assumption out of which we operate. Yet Jesus explicitly turns from this temptation. Our Father does not let himself be found in this way. After all, are we so stupid that we would not turn to God—or to anything for that matter—if it were found to pay off? If all we needed to do was say: "Okay, I'll pray to you if I can expect no disastrous illnesses, no accidents, a long prosperous life, and everything going well with the kids." But God is not a means to our ends—even good ends such as these.

Our prayers can in fact legitimately be offered for protection and help in this life. They are not to be completely banned, as we will see shortly. But there is still another subtle way in which our vulnerability does not enter into us deeply and drive out our unspoken and only half-formed assumptions. This happens when we assume that, if our prayers for help are not answered in this life, in the next world it will all be made up to us. What we do not get here, we will get in heaven. Our religion is thus used to give us consolation and to compensate us for our losses on earth. This piety, however heartfelt, may miss the gateway completely. When God fails to be a shield that wards off harm in this life, or who does not give us what we desire, true piety is not to believe that there is another world and in that world what we failed to get here will be made up to us. That is just another way of looking at God as a means for getting us what we want. To think he supplies it in the *next* life is to be no more pious than those who claim he looks after them in *this* life. Both forms of piety share the same assumptions, an assumption made even by some non-believers: namely, that God looks after us. One thinks he looks after us here; the other thinks he will look after us in heaven; the third thinks his failure to look after us proves he doesn't exist. But the assumption underlying all three is the same.

To put off being looked after until the next world, when what we expect in that next world is a compensation for the frustration of our wishes in this world, is not to know God. However much he may be talked about, thought about, or prayed to, he is not known. Even those who healed, prophesied, and cast out demons *in Christ's name* were disowned by him.

To know God is to realize that there is a felicity that is beyond pain and compensation. There is a joy that is beyond the issue of rewards to make up for loss. Paul described all his previous achievements before knowing Christ, and that were now lost, as of no account. This is not because pain and loss do not matter, but because to deal with God is to find a reality who is *incommensurate* with all the world. He is not on the same scale of measure or on the same balance as anything else; and what he wants to give us is *himself*.

Let us look more closely at this felicity or joy that we receive when he gives himself to us. The small craving, that one desire that exists buried amid our multitude of desires, of which I have already spoken, is where God touches us. It is the feeding of *that* hunger that makes us realize that the nourishment received there is incommensurate with all else that we can receive, that it is without price. It gives us a joy that is beyond the satisfaction or frustration of all the other desires we have.

C. S. Lewis's spiritual autobiography is called *Surprised by Joy*. What he received was a surprise; he did not expect it. This is not only because he was not looking for it, but because the joy of God's presence is incommensurate with all other things we know. It was the *nature* of that joy that surprised him. He suggests this by saying in one place that he could equally well have called it a kind of sorrow or grief, except that it was elevating and pervaded by a sense of peace.

We find the experience of God's presence, the nourishment of that small craving that the world cannot satisfy, portrayed in Georges Bernanos's novel *Joy*. The young girl who has this joy is clearly aware that she receives precisely and only because she is hungry. Though in a prosperous home, she realizes she has nothing because what she longs for the world cannot supply. She realizes that with this hunger she is dependent, and so she can receive.

Likewise, in still another art form, we find the same truth portrayed. As is well known, Beethoven's Ninth Symphony has a choral section in the last movement. Out of a sea of sound the very first word that thrusts itself like a massive cliff is "Joy!" To anyone who knows the felicity of God's presence, that choral outburst suggests the same reality that Paul frequently alludes to at the beginning of his letters, "Grace and peace to you from God our Father." The experience of God's presence that feeds our hunger is an experience of grace, peace, joy—a felicity the world cannot give.

Our trust in God is not to be based upon being protected from all harm, or upon having a special relationship
so that if we turn to him in earnest prayer he will give us
what we want. Our trust is not to be based upon looking
at the bright things of life, and ignoring the bad. Our trust
is not based upon a compartmentalization of the beauty,
harmony, and order we find in nature. We are not to take
the pleasantness of nature as evidence of his care and
ignore the fact that the very same laws of nature also bring
us storms, earthquakes, and drought. Nor is our trust to be
based on the misguided pious idea that, since we do not
always get what we want in this world, we will get it in the
next. We are not to look for such consolation for our pri-
vations or losses. We, who are spiritual animals, who are
vulnerable and in the thick of human misery, are to learn
that there is a reality who gives us a felicity—a joy and a
peace—unlike anything we can find. We may have this
felicity whether many of our other desires are met, or
whether many of them are frustrated. It is this felicity that
enables us to endure and to trust in his goodness.

This joy or felicity is not an esoteric mysticism. We can
receive it in such prosaic ways as hearing a hymn sung, or
thinking of some words of Jesus, or in a communion service. We find in them a nourishment for our hunger, a
nourishment that nothing else gives us. The food or the
way the food comes is prosaic and simple.

What is not so simple is getting ourselves into the condition whereby we can receive such nourishment. What is
difficult is to keep our craving for more than bread alone
from being deflected by all the ways our consciousness can
be focused on material goods. What is difficult is to learn
from suffering that we are exposed, vulnerable, and
dependent. But as we become better and better able to
receive, the more nourishment we can receive. In time we
become more and more aware of God's presence until we
find ourselves bursting out in joyful praise. That astounding felicity known by Paul and testified to in different

ways by Bernanos, C. S. Lewis, and perhaps by Beethoven, now encompasses us as well.

We can now see, without having as yet experienced this felicity ourselves, that religion is not a projection of the wishful thinking of immature people. All of us have wishes for things of this world. Many of our desires are frustrated. We can indeed be immature about our frustrations. We can try to use God as a way to avoid facing our frustration. We can, for example, look to God as one who will supply us in the next world with what we wanted but could not get in this one. If that is why we believe in God, then we are indeed immature. Such immaturity does not of course mean that we cannot grow up religiously. But to believe in God because we cannot face the reality of misfortune, injustice, or just the plain ordinary trials of being human is not to be in contact with God.

Christianity, however, is not the projection of immature people. The felicity experienced from a contact with God feeds a distinctive craving. His presence does not satisfy a hunger that *might* have been satisfied by things of this world. His presence does not serve as a substitute for various good things of this world that we did not or could not get. The small craving we have cannot be satisfied by anything of this world. No one, even those fortunate in escaping "the slings and arrows of outrageous fortune," will ever be completely satisfied by the things of this world. Mature and immature, fortunate and unfortunate are on equal footing in this respect. The felicity that is promised in religion is beyond pain, loss, and compensation because it is not within the network of the satisfaction of our desires for things of this world.

Finally we have reached the place where it becomes apparent how we can legitimately pray for God's help and protection. We can now see how we may pray to him without injury to our spiritual welfare. It is because the felicity that we may receive from him is outside the network of worldly satisfaction, beyond loss, pain, and compensation. We can and do receive in this life much consolation and help from God without harm to our spiritual welfare—that is, without its being destructive to our love for him. We can also receive by his providence protection from many ills and dangers without harm to our spiritual well-being. For in both cases we love God: we recognize his reality; we experience the joy of knowing him because he nourishes a hunger, a longing which is a desire *only for him*. We are not in danger of trying to turn him into a *means* to our ends. We can ask for and receive his protection and we can endure suffering because in both cases we love him. Thus Paul can write that nothing can separate us from the love of God—neither famine nor sword, sickness nor death (Romans 8:31–39).

Our craving for material goods and our craving for security can easily overcome us. We can be guided more than we realize by our expectation of a visible demonstration of his protection of us, and a conviction that only in this way can we believe in the reality of his love. But we can even now in that condition pray for his help. We can ask him to help us to take our concentration off of material goods. We can ask him to help us learn from suffering. We can ask him to help us, bit by bit—for none of us can ever do it all at once—face the misery that many people have suffered throughout history. We can ask for help to face our own lack of security and the vulnerability of those we love. Even before we know him, even before we have tasted that nourishment that can eventually grow into the wonderful joy of contact with his presence, we may pray for him to help us find our way to him. We may expect his help. For our prayer is guided by at least the beginning of a desire to receive him.

three

THE TEMPTATION
OF PRESTIGE

The devil took Jesus to a very high mountain and showed him the kingdoms of the world and their glory. Perhaps something of the grandeur of the scene can be imagined if you recall the sublime feeling you can get on a clear day from a high mountain, or perhaps the magnificent view from an airplane looking down on a great city. I remember very well seeing London that way once— the beautiful curve of the river passing between ancient churches and monuments, all glistening and shining in the sunlight.

The beauty of such scenes may enable us to understand why Satan, in mythology, is not always pictured as ugly and hideous, but sometimes as splendidly handsome and attractive. The ancients knew that beauty attracts us and draws us; it holds us spellbound sometimes, as, for example, in listening to great music. Evil relies on that fact; it tries to hide its own boring, tiresome, flat emptiness with a cover of glory. The best-selling novel *The Bell Jar* by Sylvia Plath has a good illustration of this sort of disguise. It is the story of some college girls who have won a contest sponsored by a glamour magazine that allows them to go to New York as junior editors for a few months, with all sorts of fringe benefits thrown in. As the novel progresses, you get behind the façade of the magazine: the glamour world it projects hides a sordid dreariness at the core.

Satan tempts Jesus to worship him, to be devoted to him, not by showing him his own true face, but by putting before Jesus the glittering grandeur of the kingdoms of this world. He hopes to attract him by hiding himself behind the radiance of these kingdoms. This should alert us to the deceptive ways in which we may be lured into evil. Evil may not show itself for what it is but instead appear as something attractive and desirable. Perhaps only when we are well caught in its whirlpool will we realize what we have done.

There is another new idea introduced with this temptation. Satan claims to be able to give Jesus the kingdoms of this world: he acts as though they are his to grant. He tells Jesus: you can rule here. This is very different from the other two temptations. For in the first Satan says to Jesus: *you* turn these stones into bread; not, let *me* do it for you. He tempts Jesus to misuse his own powers. In the second temptation, he urges Jesus to call upon *God* to protect him from harm in miraculous ways, so as to prove his claim to Messiahship. But here in the third temptation Satan reveals his own strength. *He* possesses the kingdoms of this world; he rules them, and he can convey them to those who will worship him.

What are we to make of this claim? Is it true that these kingdoms are under his control? Is not our Father, the maker of heaven and earth, the one whose providence rules all things? This is the first of several strands that we need to follow before we can discover the whole pattern. When the pattern is unfolded we will be able to recognize the powerful conflict this temptation introduces into Jesus' life and the force it exerts on our own as well.

We can begin to understand Satan's claim by recalling how nations usually operate. Nations or kingdoms customarily act out of self-interest; they fear other nations and are on their guard against them. They often assert their power to protect themselves or conquer others. Nations love glory—they parade their history and their exploits before their citizens to win allegiance and devotion. Who wants to be devoted to a loser? So nations usually try to come out on top and keep others in check, either by sheer strength, or if they are small, by making alliances with greater powers. If there is no way to overcome the obvious frailty of a nation, you can always make a cult of righteous self-pity out of the way your nation has been an innocent victim of vicious greater powers. This tale is nearly always plausible because there is rarely a shortage of crimes between nations.

Many of us want our nation to operate on the basis of justice, respect for others, and good will, and not on a basis of sheer self-interest and the pursuit of glory, as did nearly all empires of the past. There is a strong desire, as evidenced by the League of Nations and its successor the United Nations, to bring a rule of law to international dealings. But our national policies are even at best only a mixture—of fear, self-aggrandizement, and fair play. So often our best intentions must, we believe, give way to realism because other nations ruthlessly pursue their interest at our expense. It is a realm of power or might where frequently, when a decision must be made, idealism and moral virtues get crowded out by necessity.

And this affects all of us, since our individual economic welfare and personal safety are largely at the mercy of political circumstances. The livelihood of North American fishermen has been hurt by the overfishing of foreigners in areas near our coast over which no one has political sovereignty. Industries geared to defense production open and close, expand and contract with terrible swiftness in various communities, bringing great prosperity or creating serious unemployment. We as individuals may thereby prosper or suffer irrespective of our personal moral worth. Whether a war breaks out while we are of military age, whether we die or survive in war, either directly by violence or indirectly by disease or hunger, bears little relation to our personal virtue. Necessities forced on nations by the rule of might, and the way this affects us individually, are largely matters of chance. As the Scriptures put it, in God's world the sun rises on the evil and the good, and rain falls on the just and unjust.

There is, then, a large part of our life that is affected by forces—both political and economic—over which we personally have no control and which have nothing to do with our personal virtues. In this domain where force rules, Satan sees an opportunity. Or to put it less poetically, in those places where our life is affected by political and economic might, we can be tempted into evil.

One way we can be tempted into evil is by our social position. If our lot in life is fortunate, we may fail to realize how much our social position and success depends on political and economic circumstances over which we personally have no control. Our position is never fully earned. No matter how hard we work, many circumstances may make it impossible to attain a prosperous position. We have already illustrated this with the example of defense industries where the opportunity of prosperity or hardship comes or goes by decisions made in places beyond our personal reach. The social position of all of us is vulnerable to rapid inflation or deflation. In Germany in the 1920s millions of middle and upper class people, some of them of great talent and ability, were impoverished, and many never recovered. The Great Depression in America is still remembered for turning professors into street-cleaners and businessmen into beggars waiting in line for free soup. When times are good, we do not often notice how vulnerable we all are. We also may fail in good times to be sufficiently aware that many who are relatively unsuccessful or even very badly off may be victims of circumstances over which they had no control. Their social status does not necessarily reflect their personal merits or demerits any more than our own status does.

Social position tempts us into evil because it tends to make us think it is an accurate measure of worth. There is a temptation for us all to estimate the value of ourselves and other people according to our respective social position. Without realizing it we often allow this social measure to tell us how highly we ought to think of ourselves or others. The social categories of the day tend to be used to tell us who and what we are, who and what others are. They are used to establish our identity.

But such a gauge is not an accurate measure of our own true value, whether it registers high or low. It is not a sound measure of the true importance of others. It does not take into account political and economic circumstances over which none of us individually has full control. These are a major factor in determining the social position we may have attained or have failed to attain. We are tempted to forget this. When we do there are several undesirable consequences. First, we become unable to find out what our own true value is; for in a way yet to be revealed to us in our pilgrimage, what we are to be is hidden with God. It is to be found only after we have passed through the gateway. That is, it is to be found only after we realize the inaccuracy of the social gauge. To think that our present identity as defined by our society is our true one keeps us from finding the true life God has in store for us. No matter how high we are, it is less than what God has planned.

Another consequence is that the social measure of importance may blind us to the genuine merits and value we and other people have. We can become enclosed in the outlook of our society. We can let it create a barrier between us and others, so that the rung on the social ladder we occupy separates us from those below and those above by absolute degrees of merit. There are differences between people, but, as we will see, they need not create a sense of separation. Reliance on the social categories of the day as a *true* measure of worth and personal identity creates barriers between us; it separates us into those who are significant, and those who are not.

Still another consequence of this social evaluation is that it becomes a powerful force in driving us. We all rightly want to be well thought of; we all rightly wish to have our worth recognized and respected. But too often we seek to realize these desires by moving up the social ladder as though it were the ladder of true self-fulfillment. Our legitimate desire for self-respect may then become a slave driver. We push ourselves to achieve our goals; we become miserable over our failures. Our minds become full of our own interests to the exclusion of others. We may desire so much to achieve that we not only neglect others but positively injure them. Other people's wishes, needs, and desires are subordinate to our own need to establish ourselves. Our desire for success is not balanced by a recognition that other people are seeking to establish their own worth as well. The need for social position thus becomes a force, a force that drives us. It threatens to gain control of us, and makes us less and less aware of the needs of others. It creates the kind of competition that puts insuperable barriers between us.

Many of us probably have some misgivings about a life of self-assertion, about the struggle to establish our own worth by trying to move up the social ladder. We understand the misery caused by failure to move up, or to move up fast enough or far enough, and we have some awareness that social status is an inaccurate measure of true worth. Yet this awareness does not free us of the power of social status because too often competition and its rewards are glamorized. There are many stories about people who have achieved great things by immense personal effort. Some of these stories are true and many such people deserve our respect. What is wrong with these stories is not so much what they say as what they *don't*. They give praise to the successful, admiration to winners, *without any thought for those who did not make it*. Only those few who succeed get praise; the large number of others are ignored. This is not fair, and its unfairness is easily seen with one of the most carefully administered college awards, a Rhodes Scholarship to Oxford.

To win this scholarship a person must survive a long process of elimination. It begins with a competition between the most able students of a particular university. One or more are selected to represent their college or university before a state selection committee. Each committee interviews all the candidates from its own state, and each state committee selects only two people. These state nominees then compete in a region made up of no fewer than six states for the four scholarships allotted to that region. Not only are these state nominees all very able people, but there is no real difference or at best only a very slight one between the person who is finally ranked as number 4 and gets a scholarship, and the person who is ranked number 5, and does not. The fourth and fifth ranked people are virtually identical in merit. Yet number 4 gets a two-year scholarship to Oxford, and is known for life as a Rhodes Scholar. Number 5 gets reimbursed for travel expenses to and from the town in which the final selection committee interviewed. The actual difference between these two, a successful and an unsuccessful candidate, is at best very slight; yet the difference in recognition and reward is enormous. The relative status conferred on the successful or unsuccessful candidate is not an accurate measure of actual merit.

This happens in many places in our society—not only in schools, but in sports and business as well. Recognition for achievement must always be made with a consciousness of the inevitable imbalance between rewards and actual merit. Otherwise the achievements are glamorized and the truth about people is suppressed.

The inaccuracy of our way of measuring personal worth can be masked in still another way. The distinction between people's importance is often justified in America by saying that there is equality of opportunity, or at least more than in most countries. This suggests that differences between people's achievements are by and large based on merit. It may indeed be true for some of us that opportunity in America is equal or at least abundant. But this can very easily keep us from realizing that the unsuccessful are separated from us in many cases by no more than chance. As we have seen, neither the relatively successful nor the relatively unsuccessful have anything to do with whether a major government contract is awarded to their town. But there is a more general factor at work. We have nothing to do with whether we are lucky or unlucky enough to be looking for our first job in good times or slack times. Also, to be in an age group that had a low birthrate, followed ten years later by an age group that had a high birthrate, as was the case with me, is to have an advantage all your life. There are always fewer contemporaries competing for positions, and you are competing at a time when the larger population younger than your own age group creates heavier demands, larger markets, and hence more job opportunities for your group in everything from teaching to car production. We do not all by any means have the same opportunities.

This may affect us in two ways. If we are relatively unsuccessful, we may become bitter, especially if we have had many bad breaks. We may be tempted to be unconcerned with other people's welfare. We have had it tough, so what do we care? We may at one time in our life have tried to be fair to others, but it did us no good. Our world has not been easy and this has hardened us to others. We then fail even to try to treat other people fairly; we do not react to them as people. We may do something for someone else, but only because it suits us. Because we have had a raw deal, we join the kingdom of might. That kingdom of political, economic, and social force often ignores our personal merit. Without realizing it, we have become a victim of the kingdom of might by letting the way it has hurt us change us into its likeness—it has made us blind to people. We fail to temper our power—however small—by any sense of obligation to others. We sense no obligation to be fair to our bosses, to our customers, to our subordinates. We do what we *have* to do, not what we ought to do. Force has turned us into things. Things act, as does every particle in the universe, by necessity and compulsion. Things do not act by a recognition of value. Only a person can do that. We have become a thing by doing no more than we must. We do not respond to what is good and treat people according to what they rightly deserve.

If, on the other hand, we are relatively successful, we may fail to see how near we are to the relatively unsuccessful. We are closer to those with less status than the places we occupy suggest. In some instances there may be no difference in merit at all. The decisive factor may be, for example, luck—the chance circumstance in which each of us was born—one in a small age group, another in a large one. We allow the kingdom of might to include us whenever we fail to see the inaccuracy of the social gauge of merit and let it dominate our attitudes toward others and ourselves.

We have seen some ways social status is not an accurate gauge of our own true worth or that of others. To find our true selves—the persons we can be when free of distorted social estimates—we may with profit examine the path of Jesus, and thereby uncover a path that we too may follow. Let us see the way Jesus responded to this temptation.

When Satan showed Jesus the kingdoms of this world and their glory, he offered him success and the prestige that goes with it. He was offering the highest social recognition possible; Jesus was to be Lord of all earthly king-doms, and to enjoy prestige, deference, and acclaim. But the glory he was being offered was one based on the use of force. As we have seen, the kingdoms of this world rely on force to get their own way and to avoid succumbing to the will of others. Their glory has as its foundation their power to get their own way, to subordinate others to their own will. He rejected such a glory. He rejected a social status that was based on might.

Perhaps his lack of sufficient status to gain acceptance by the Jewish leaders is reflected in the comments of his detractors who said, "'Is not this the carpenter, the son of Mary and brother of James and Joses and Judas and Simon, and are not his sisters here with us?' And they took offense at him" (Mark 6:3). Jesus apparently felt the lowliness of his position, when he said, "Foxes have holes, and birds of the air have nests; but the Son of man has nowhere to lay his head" (Matt. 8:20).

The attractiveness of social prestige may have had its pull on Jesus. Nonetheless, the main attractiveness of Satan's offer was not the prestige that goes with success, but success itself. Jesus' mission was to enable people to find the kingdom of God. But how was this to be achieved? How was he to win people over? How was he to save us?

When the Father created the universe and decided to make spirits who could be like himself—creative, with imagination, capable of moral insight, and of spontaneous devotion—he faced a dilemma. He faced the problem of allowing people freedom, or to use his power in such a way as to compel them to recognize his sovereignty. The great-est and first commandment of the universe is that only God is to be worshiped; only he is the foundation and fountain of life. But how is that commandment to be kept? By force? By punishment when we do not turn to him, so that it becomes obvious that it pays to worship God? (Would that even be devotion? Wholehearted attachment?) Or by God's restricting himself, by pulling back on the exercise of his power, by limiting himself, and letting us seek him because of our hunger, because we have learned to love him? This is a terrible choice because it means exposing creatures to awful suffering—to all the ills and torments and ravages that our history and life are full of. It is to expose us to evil, to rampant and hidden evil that can destroy us utterly. We know what our Father chose to do.

Jesus in the wilderness faced this temptation: to accept or to deny God's choice. He was faced with accepting the suffering, the brutality, the evil of people; or to refuse to accept it, and to *impose* himself on people. He could use the devil's way: maximization of power—use all you have got to get your own way, no matter how you do it. And that is a temptation because the end was good: to stop people's suffering, to stop their wandering in darkness, to end the terrible beastliness and destruction that plagues us.

In Dostoyevsky's "Grand Inquisitor" the Inquisitor has so much compassion for people that he uses power and deception to alleviate their suffering. The Grand Inquisitor and Jesus are both moved to help people by compassion, but they use different methods. The one uses power to compel obedience; Jesus uses truth and love to elicit our willing obedience.

It is not an easy choice. So much so that later in his life Jesus weeps over Jerusalem, "O Jerusalem, Jerusalem, killing the prophets and stoning those who are sent to you! How often would I have gathered your children together as a hen gathers her brood under her wings, and you would not!" (Matt. 23:37).

Jesus painfully and faithfully shows the same kind of compassion, the same kind of restraint, as his Father does. He does not try to use force any more than his Father does in order to get his way. And Jesus suffers the consequences of his renunciation in at least three ways. First, he suffers in sorrow at the failure of many to follow the path he opens up, as we saw in the passage about his weeping over Jerusalem. Second, by his renunciation of might, he renounces the social prestige that goes with its successful use. We see echoes of the pain this caused in his comment about having no place to lay his head. He has to bear the contempt of his detractors who jeer at him as the son of a carpenter. The third consequence only becomes apparent near the end of his life. His lack of social position and physical might make it possible for others to use force against him. So he not only rejects might as the basis of his life's work, but is willing to become its victim on the cross.

He accepts his Father's way because he knows what effects force has on people. When Satan shows him the kingdoms of the world and their glory, Jesus recognizes behind the façade of glory the ugliness of the kingdom of might. Might has the effect of a cold frost that, when it touches living plants, withers them and permanently scars them with blackness. When we use force to get our own way, we transform people into things. They cease to be people when their wishes and legitimate desires have no effect on us. When, on the other hand, we encounter each other with a desire to be fair, do we not enter into a new kind of reality? We seem to be enveloped by a mystery in which we both participate. It comes into being merely from the desire to be fair. But introduce force, introduce the desire to get our own way by might, and it vanishes abruptly. We now have only the clash of things, not the meeting of persons.

Mystery withers at the very touch of force. This is a law, a truth that governs us as firmly as any law we have met so far, and as firmly as any that exists in all the permutations of matter and energy. When we treat other people as objects subordinate to our goals, their mystery has no effect on us. The larger mystery into which genuine personal encounter can lead us never becomes open to us.

We thereby lose one of the ways into the new kind of reality that Jesus desired that we find.

Force not only closes us off from this reality but it is an evil that leaves its scars on people; it marks them like a blight. Even if a plant should survive, its darkened and blunted stems often never wholly come back. Force can never be exercised without leaving permanent damage. Those who went through the Great Depression have never forgotten the humiliation of being reduced to beggars. Refugees whose experiences verge on Christ's humiliation and those who survived the concentration camps do not walk scot-free of the effects of such outrageous treatment.

All of us bear the aftermarks of evil to some degree. Our lives are pit-marked by the humiliations we receive when others refuse to be fair to us or insist on getting their own way at our expense. Think of the way fathers- or mothers-in-law often distrust their children's marriage partner. Often the son- or daughter-in-law is judged not good enough by very severe and unfair standards. This is felt, and is destructive. On the other hand, think how in-laws are regarded as "things" that keep interfering and judging. Most likely, they are simply trying to help their (now married) child—their motive is love—but this laudable motive goes unnoticed. These subtle effects of our power on each other close us off from each other, and they leave their scars and marks on us.

From such suffering—whether extreme or very ordinary—we have the opportunity to learn in a concrete way of the need for justice. Suffering can make us realize for ourselves how much forgiveness and reconciliation are needed in all human affairs. It can bring home to us that familiar passage from Micah, "What does the LORD require of you, but to do justice, and to love mercy, and to walk humbly with your God?" (6:8b).

This passage teaches us to avoid force and it also shows the way to overcome its effects and even to remove its scars. Whether we are above or below others we are to seek to be fair, and not to get our own way at others' expense. If we are below we are not to become hardened and indifferent; to think, "To hell with the boss. To hell with the company." If we have considerable social status, we are to remember that as we would be treated by our Lord, so let us be thoughtful of those beneath us. To act fairly, to be merciful, and to seek reconciliation open us up to a different world. We can see it more and more clearly as we leave the world of might. We can feel and experience it more vividly as we progressively leave behind the world of getting our own way.

How beautiful it is that Jesus chose to live in the realm of justice, the realm of forgiveness, and the realm of reconciliation. He would not use might. He would not call on legions of angels to get his own way. He teaches and heals. In his acts of forgiveness and compassion he shows us what is good; and he asks us to hear of God's mercy as good news. But he never imposes himself on anyone. On the contrary, he not only rejects force as a means, but, as we have said, he suffers and endures the effects of force on himself.

Jesus did, however, have status. He had the status of Lord. But his lordship was not based on force, like that of most earthly rulers. His was based on his justice, his mercy, and his humility before the Father (in that he obeyed, not his own, but his Father's will). He was elevated because he followed that path to greatness. Justice, mercy, humility form a path that does not divide us or set us apart but that creates and promotes community between us. It enriches us all by giving us access to each other across the barriers of social position. It heals the withering effects of force. We see it in operation throughout Jesus' life. He was oblivious to the barriers created by social status. He made some who were lowly, like fishermen, and even social outcasts, like the tax-collector Matthew, his disciples. He ate with publicans and sinners, and showed compassion throughout his life to the poor. He was bringing a different kind of kingdom to us and making it available.

Yet each of us very much likes to get our own way. We often strive very hard to make things come out as we want. When they don't, sometimes we get furious, or perhaps depressed. Sometimes we feel that life is unfair and that this is a terrible world. Getting our own way looks beautiful, looks glorious, because it is so full of ourselves. Could this be the secret attraction of force? Our own person expands to the extent we are effective in getting what we want. But to be fair, we have to pull ourselves back, to restrain ourselves by recognition of another person. People in front of us in a long line, especially when we are in a hurry, often make us feel full of hatred. But should a friend let us go through a side-door, we would be filled with a surge of pleasure. Other people limit us; fairness limits us. Often we experience or feel this in our anger, hatred, frustration, and depression. Yet we cannot encounter other people *as people* unless we strive to be fair. We cannot encounter them as mysteries that enable us to find and live in a new kind of reality. Everywhere we turn, we meet people; and in every relation we have the opportunity to be fair. When we persistently try to be fair, we start to enter a realm that is unlike that of the kingdom of might. The kingdom of trying to get our own way is where we usually live, and from it we reap its fruits—at first pleasant ones; only later do they grow bitter.

Fairness also leads us to recognize the need for forgiveness. In the case of the mutual injustice between in-laws, if both sides seek to be fair, each will come to recognize how unfair they have been to each other. How horrible their acts and thoughts then look. When such recognition takes place, only forgiveness or mercy can enable contact to be re-opened, and contact at a newer and richer level. Finally, fairness and forgiveness together have the effect of rendering us humble. It now becomes less and less of a strain to encounter other people as people; for there is so much less of ourselves protruding for them to bump against and cause pain. No longer is getting our own way spread out so far. Our false overextension is trimmed back, and we now can enter more easily into community. Each time we respect each other as people, we become more able to give and to receive without resentment.

We have now found that the final arch of the gateway to the reality of God is barred by our own person. It is I myself who stand in the way. What I need to give up in order to receive a fuller life—to live in contact with the true world and the Spirit of God—is myself. More accurately, it is my false overexpanded self that must be shed. The dissolving of our false selves enables what we are and what we are to become to emerge.

There are, as we have seen, at least two factors that keep each of us from this truer life. First, the desire to get our own way without limit, to expand ourselves as far as possible. It is obvious that none of us can get our own way without limit. Yet is not such a desire secretly at work in you? Is it perhaps not at the root of some of your anger, your frustration, your depression, your anxiety? Is it perhaps not at the root of some of your elation, your pleasure, your self-satisfaction? Does it not perhaps cut you off from a closeness, from a contact with some people? Few, if any, of us, are fully free of the effects of the desire to get our own way, even if we have made some progress in overcoming it.

Although other people do limit and restrict us by interfering with our desires, they also give us an opportunity. They give us the opportunity to start the long but meaningful process of shrinking the unrealistic overextension of ourselves. They thereby give us the opportunity to find ourselves. For there are two different ways in which our limitations come home to us. One is through the frustration of our desires. This is followed by dozens and dozens of ways of trying to handle our frustration—from daydreaming to depression, from escapism to fury. The second way our limits come home to us is when we see other people as realities that have a legitimate claim on us. When we restrict *ourselves because we respect others,* our falseness, our overexpanded self, begins to fall away. Each such encounter helps to erode it. As time goes on, we start to experience for ourselves the fact that other people's legitimate claims on us, which we used to find so frustrating, have led to our transformation. They have enabled us to experience the joy of entering into a different kind of world.

We really do live in a different kind of world and we ourselves are different, fuller lands of people when we leave the kingdom of might. When we start to shed that secret, powerful desire to get our own way without limit, we enter the kingdom of fairness, forgiveness, and humility. To say we thereby become *more* is misleading. We do not add to what we *were.* Instead, we have begun to be transformed. We have started to live more truly because we live closer to the truth about ourselves and other people.

We also saw a second factor at work that hindered the emergence of our true self. All of us have worth. We rightly desire to develop ourselves and to have our worth recognized by others. But we may understand what we are and what we are to become by our society's estimation of importance and significance. Now the social standards of our society are not completely erroneous; they do take some account of people's merits. But they are very distorted, and too hit-and-miss to be an accurate gauge, as we have tried to show with some examples.

When we fail to see how much our own social status is a product of chance, we are under an illusion. Our true self cannot appear, grow, and develop because of a picture given to us by the social measure. Even if we are very illustrious, the highest social prestige cannot measure the person we are to become when we are related to God and live with each other free of the kingdom of might.

Another aspect of our social bondage is when we allow social position to be the judge of *other* people's significance and value. We then fail to perceive the bond that exists between us and all people, whatever our status. For there is a bond between us all that is created by the fact that all of us are vulnerable to political and economic upheaval. Human suffering caused by political and economic events over which we have no personal control and which are oblivious to personal merits can open us up to a sense of community. Suffering can enable us to reach across all social barriers. We can become free of the inaccuracies of social valuation and know that social status is based to a large degree on chance. We still realize people are different; but differences do not prevent us from recognizing a bond. All of us have an essential way in which we are equal despite all differences that separate us—our liability to misfortune. Chance can reduce any of us to poverty, or even to a battered piece of lifeless matter, through no particular fault of our own.

As we become freer of the illusions created by our false self-expansion and our social self, we are able to look elsewhere for our true identity. We are more able to receive the elevation God seeks to confer on us; for as Paul has written, what we are to be is hid with God. It is, as we will see shortly, revealed to us bit by bit after we emerge from this gateway.

We are able to move through this gateway, able to follow Jesus, the more we are able to be like him. For that humble man of Galilee recognized what forceful self-expansion was and its withering effects. He understood its utter indifference to people as people. He refused to be its servant or slave, and he showed compassion to its victims. Not only did he not seek to get his own way by might, but he did not accept what his society said he was or said anyone else was either. By these renunciations, he pioneered a way to the Father, telling us, "He who loves his life loses it, and he who hates his life in this world will keep it for eternal life" (John 12:25).

Part 2

STEPS ALONG
THE WAY

Jesus said, "The gate is narrow and the way is hard that leads to life" (Matt. 7:14). The three temptations Christ endured in the wilderness reveal how very narrow indeed the gateway is that leads to the reality of God. But we should not be discouraged. There are several reasons for us to continue trying.

First, we just cannot stand still where we now are. We do not have a bird in hand that we are being asked to release in order to catch two in the bush. We do not have complete control of our lives or our possessions. There is a drift in life whose effects even the most self-directed person cannot completely overcome. We are subject not only to aging and death, but to illness and accident. We are not at any time in a position of impregnable security, able to have our bird in hand without having to take any risks. We cannot just sit tight; we are in motion. So to be realistic we ought to be concerned about the direction of our movement.

Second, our life is also in motion because we seek a fuller life. Even if we never change our job or move from our neighborhood, we sense a yearning for more than we have and to be more than we are. For this reason, we feel the attraction of material goods, security, and the glory of earthly success. But we may also sometimes feel a counter attraction. We feel pulled in different directions; for we at times deeply feel, without necessarily being able to say it, that we cannot find fullness of life in material goods, security, or the glory of earthly success. This conflict, which is unpleasant, is really a good sign. One way in which God's reality approaches us is when we feel these counter pulls. The very disquiet we feel ought to encourage us. It means we have not gone completely astray. Even though we have not conquered or fully surmounted the temptations of material goods, security, and earthly success, as long as we continue to feel a counter pull, we are moving—even if only slowly and in a zigzag way—in the right direction.

Third, as we move toward God, we find our true selves. Our true self comes to us as we search for a spiritual realm, as we search for God. So the renunciations we make are not *goals*. They are *means* leading to fullness of life. Our self-deflation and self-discipline enable a life, more precious and lovely than we have ever known, to emerge. It is a life penetrated by the divine presence. Our self-deflation is accompanied by a simultaneous openness to the life God seeks to give us. And we are continually given the strength to shed what is false in our lives for what is true by God's secret presence within us. His presence, at first experienced by us perhaps only in the conflict and counter pull we have described, is quietly growing in us. It increases without our awareness. Then one day we start to become aware that we have already begun to receive the life God seeks us to have.

So we are now ready to go forward, even though we have not perfectly overcome the temptations that form the gateway into a new reality. Our hunger for more than material goods, which keeps mysteriously reappearing; our growing ability to face human suffering openly and to learn from it; our striving to be more fair and the resulting awareness of the need for forgiveness, all conspire to move us toward a different world and into a new reality. Our pilgrimage now starts to enter a new phase. The person we are to become—the person that Paul said was hid with God—now starts to emerge. Bit by bit what we are to be and the life we are to lead starts to be revealed. It is much more than we can take in all at once. So we must receive it and become it in stages. We must, in other words, take some steps, some steps along the way to our final destination.

At this stage in our pilgrimage, we shall have some new guides. We will be able to discern the path Christ pioneered for us by following in the footsteps of some of his early followers. They followed him, and we will be able to follow him by walking in their footsteps. The steps we are to make in our pilgrimage are revealed to us by Mary, the mother of Jesus; by the shepherds and wise men of the Christmas story; and by Peter, who was called the rock. Each of them shows us a different step along the way, a step that moves us deeper into the reality of God and simultaneously allows more of our true self and our true worth to emerge. One other revealing step along the way calls on us to look at our own talents and abilities, especially the way they both disappoint us and also tempt us to try to be self-sufficient.

In these four steps along the way, our understanding of humility is deepened. For what we are to be is a gift. It takes humility to receive such a gift. So humility is not one virtue among many others. It is the condition for *becoming* religious; it is the condition for receiving the mystery of God and thereby finding our own true selves.

Yet humility, for all its importance, is one of the least understood spiritual conditions. We think of humble people as doormats, as milk toasts, as drab personalities. But we may have already sensed how inaccurate this is by our wrestling with the temptations. We begin to be humble as we recognize that fullness of life cannot be found in bread alone, but is a mystery beyond our control. We become progressively more humble as we more deeply feel that full security is not within our grasp. Our sense of humility expands as we sense the inadequacy of measuring human worth by social position. It grows, without our consciousness, as we seek to be fair, and renounce the glory based on getting our own way by might. A humble person may thus be quite lively and very active. Personality traits such as introvert-extrovert, active-passive, optimistic-pessimistic are irrelevant to whether a person is fair or compassionate. It is by the latter traits that humility is characterized.

So the steps we are now to take are a movement into greater humility. We become better able to receive the astounding elevation that God seeks to give us. Each step into humility is a movement toward a great reversal: the change from shrinking, which we find painful, into the joy of fullness and elevation.

This spiritual paradox is beautifully captured in a story G. K. Chesterton tells us he learned in his nursery. He used the story to explain the spiritual change that happens in many lives. He said, "My nurse once told me that if you start digging down toward the center of the earth and keep on going, after a certain point, you won't be digging downwards anymore but digging upwards." Humility at first involves shrinkage of our overextended selves, but it is only a prelude to fullness and elevation. It is this spiritual paradox that we are now ready to enter for ourselves.

four

COMMON
DECENCY

E veryday experience suggests that it is easy to receive
and hard to give. I do not wish to minimize the difficulties in giving, but the three temptations we have
encountered have already suggested to us how difficult it
is to receive God's presence. This is not because God
withholds himself or hides from us. It is largely because we
are in the wrong shape. Water poured on a flat piece of
metal just spills off. But if poured into metal of the proper
shape, it will stay. Our personal lives need to be shaped so
we can receive his presence. As we have seen, our shaping
begins with the temptation to seek fullness of life from
material goods. It is painful to realize that we do not live
by bread alone, and to resist trying to satisfy that extra
hunger with material goods. It takes an effort to admit that
there is nothing we know of that could fill us. It hurts to
remain empty and to allow that emptiness to expand and
shape us. The same painful shaping process takes place
with the other two temptations, as we have seen.

But now we encounter a new barrier to receiving. This
one springs out of the very greatness of the gift itself. The

presence of God is so elevating, gives us such honor, that we often are too small to receive it. It is so great that we cannot hold it, at least not all at once. We can recognize our limitations and how to handle them by looking at Mary, the mother of Jesus. She is the perfect example of how we are to receive our elevation.

For Roman Catholics, Mary is the Blessed Virgin Mary; for Eastern Orthodox, she is the Mother of God; for all other Christians, she is an embarrassment. Protestants do not know what to do with her. To Protestants, of course, she is important because she is the mother of Jesus. Because Jesus had a mother we see that he is indeed fully human. His identification with us is also shown by his acceptance of human duties, such as the consideration he showed to his mother even from the cross when he commended her to the care of John. But Jesus' humanity does not tell us why Mary is to be honored. It does not tell us why the Bible says that "henceforth all generations will call me blessed." It is by understanding this elevation that we can understand how Mary is a perfect example of how we are to receive God's love.

Among many Protestants, I expect, the main function of Mary is as a test case for biblical infallibility. "Do you believe in the virgin birth?" it is asked. If you don't, then it is claimed you do not believe in the authority of the Bible.

Aside from the fact that this is not a valid argument, how does this honor Mary? If we want a way to check people out on biblical authority, why not ask: "Do you believe an angel appeared to Mary?" This would do just as well as the question, "Do you believe in the virgin birth?" Mary is not honored by using her to trip people up.

One Protestant who did honor Mary was Kierkegaard. Mary, he said, had great faith. She believed the angel's announcement. This is true. Mary did have great faith. This is utterly clear in the Scriptures. Just notice the contrast between Mary and Zechariah. Just before the story about Mary, we have that of Zechariah. Zechariah's wife Elizabeth was barren. They had had no children and they were advanced in years. While Zechariah was in the Temple, Gabriel appeared to him and announced that his wife would conceive and bear a son, who was to be called John. John, later known as John the Baptist, was to prepare the way for the Lord. Zechariah did not believe Gabriel. So he was struck dumb, unable to speak, until after the angel's words had come true.

Zechariah did not believe; Mary did. Mary replied to the angel, "Behold, I am the handmaid of the Lord; let it be to me according to your word." Later Elizabeth said of Mary, "Blessed is she who believed."

Mary indeed had great faith and is called blessed because of it. She deserves to be honored for it. But this is not enough to account for her place in Scripture. It is not enough to account for why it is written, "henceforth all generations will call me blessed." We can see this by a brief look at Joseph. When he learned that Mary, his betrothed, was with child, he was troubled. But when an angel in a dream told him that Mary's child was of God, he *believed*. He too had great faith. Yet Joseph, who is indeed honored in Scripture, is much less honored than Mary. Both had great faith; both are honored, but why Mary so much more?

We come to the most obvious reason. Not only did she have great faith, but she bore the Christ child. Of all the women in Israel, of all the women in creation, this humble maiden of Nazareth was selected to bear the Christ child. She was to be the one to nurse him, to rock him to sleep, to be bound to him as no other mortal creature can be bound: to be mother to him. This is indeed enough to make us stand in awe before Mary: for he who is mighty has indeed done great things for her. He has singled her out from all creatures for ever and ever.

And yet, there is still another reason, a greater reason than all these—a reason found in Mary's own words. They are recorded in Luke and are nowadays called the *Magnificat*. They form a song Mary sings to praise the Lord for what he has done. In what Mary says the Lord has done, we find the culmination of all the reasons she is to be honored. It gathers up all the other reasons and sits mounted on them like a radiant diamond in the crown of a ring.

Mary, a simple village girl, realized with perfect clarity and to a perfect degree *how to receive* Christ. She saw that Christ's coming meant that the proud had been passed over, and he had come to a lowly maiden. She saw that the mighty had been put down from their thrones, and those of low degree exalted. She saw that the hungry are to be filled with good things; the rich to be sent away emptyhanded. The system of values and social worth whereby the proud, mighty, and rich are apart and above, and do not recognize kinship with people below, is utterly rejected.

Mary understood the gospel: she perceived immediately what it meant. She saw what it meant that Christ was to be born of her, a lowly peasant. She understood what her elevation meant.

Now we can see the great diamond, the jewel that shines here with such radiance. Mary, who is elevated, remains humble. Her elevation did not create a barrier between her and others so that they became her servants. She, who is honored above all women, did not become proud. She is known to the disciples and the early Christian believers as one who bore the Christ child but who remained humble. She not only understood the gospel, she lived it.

Had she not remained lowly, she would not have received the Christ. She would indeed have been his physical mother, but she would not have received her elevation. She would have corrupted it. To receive him means that a person no longer seeks to stand over others. We can feel significant and important, we can deeply and truly feel our worth and preciousness, without standing over anyone, without putting anyone down. For we are elevated into a community in which each one gives and receives, and where differences do not cut us off from each other. Christ came to put down the mighty—not so that the lowly might stand on top of them; for a mere reversal of the denominator and numerator in human affairs is not good news. Instead, Christ eliminated the entire arrangement in which value and worth require social humiliation.

We see this emphasized by the episode in which Jesus' disciples were involved in a dispute over greatness, or as we would put it, over the question, Who is important? James and John had asked that when Jesus came into his glory they might have the places of honor, one at his right hand and the other at his left. When the other ten disciples heard of it, they were furious. James and John had beaten them to the draw. Jesus then explained to all that importance is indeed ordinarily based on having others subordinate to your will and wishes, but that this is not his measure of greatness or worth. Instead of being served—having others do your will—he commands them to serve others. This is in imitation of himself, who "came not to be served, but to serve, and to give his life as a ransom for many" (Matt. 20:28).

That we are to serve indicates that others are *worthy* of our concern and effort, worthy of our regard and attention. It also means that we ourselves are worthy of the care and concern of others. So that what is offered is community, one of mutual recognition of one another's significance and concern for one another.

To receive the love of God, to receive his concern, to receive his recognition of our worth and preciousness, to receive his forgiveness and invitation to live in communion now and forever, is to have our elevation become a reason to serve others. To react thus to the elevation God gives us is a sign that we have indeed actually received his love. It is one of the steps along the way. To receive is to be made progressively free of the tenacity of our desire, like that desire we see in the disciples, to stand over others, to have others serve our wishes, our goals, our ambitions; to overcome our desire for height, for prestige at others' expense.

Let me illustrate with a specific case what it means to overcome our distorted views of what people are worth. The illustration is based on a novel by Iris Murdoch called *Bruno's Dream*.

The novel opens with Bruno bedridden, slowly dying of old age, and ends with his passing into oblivion. He has never cut a big figure in life, either in his work or as a husband and parent. His only notable achievements were his love and knowledge of spiders, and his affection for a valuable stamp collection that he inherited. Now that he is old and dying, he is even more socially marginal. He cannot make a ripple even in his little world. Yet the novelist suggests that a centrally significant activity is taking place as his body slowly undergoes biological decay. For at times he engages in a silent dialogue with himself, recalling the "dream" that was his life, especially his unsatisfactory relationship with his now dead wife. What had gone wrong? What had she wanted to tell him at the end when she called to him so frantically and he had avoided coming until it was too late? What had she really been like? Now, removed from her presence, he is able to seek with some detachment to understand their relationship, and indeed to understand the person that he himself is.

The search is not performed particularly well. It has no social consequences; it has no effects even in his immediate household. But it matters. A person is finding out who another person was, and who he himself is. If people matter, it matters to know them more truly, even if they are dead. If we ourselves matter, it matters to know ourselves more truly, even when we are dying. Bruno's example shows us that this important search can be carried out even in very confined circumstances.

Bruno's only financial value is his stamp collection. Yet he receives care that is considerate, even compassionate, from those who have no expectation of reward (and in fact after all possibility of reward is removed by the accidental destruction of the collection). His physical repulsiveness, his growing inability to recognize anyone, much less be grateful to them, does not prevent his daughter-in-law from looking after him right to the end. He is a unique person, for those who can see him, and calls for compassionate care. He is perhaps below the level that immediately evokes our pity, but his daughter-in-law can see him as a person and not be blinded by his lack of monetary value or his physical repulsiveness.

The novelist shows us how we are to treat people by making the central character of her novel a socially marginal person. We see what it is to recognize a person's worth; we see that recognition means service. It means common decency. Such care is done for its own sake: not for its results, but because particular people matter. This conviction that people matter is behind much of the work of the church: showing compassion to the elderly, the dying, the neglected retarded child and adult. This work may not increase church membership or necessarily have any financial benefit. It is done for the sake of the people themselves.

This is why Mary is honored so much. She immediately understood what the disciples did not understand, and she was able to live it. To receive God's love, which does not match our social position or prestige but exceeds it however high it might be, is to recognize that the social measure of people has been set aside by God. God's love above all rejects the idea on which social prestige operates, that greatness is to have others subordinate to yourself. To receive our elevation from God—to receive God's love—is to be able both to recognize and to live this transformation.

God's love is more than we can receive at once. But we can start from where we are. Mary is the great example for us to follow because she shows us how we can receive the Christ. Just as she was elevated, so too are we. We, who are but dust and ashes, belonging to the kingdom of social worth, are called to be sons and daughters of the most high. We are to dwell on high with him forever and ever. And yet like Mary who is elevated, we are to remain humble. Though she was blessed above women, she did not ask to be carried about and given deference as a queen by the disciples and other followers of Jesus. She performed the services of child-bearing and child-rearing, cooking, and sewing. Not that there is a divine calling to "woman's work" in this; but whatever work a follower of Christ is called to do, it is to serve others. We are called out of a life in which our worth is based on self-aggrandizement and self-expansion. Whatever our job or work is, at the bottom it is to be guided by the same ideal—the service of other people because they are people.

Christians are people who seek to bear in mind always their infinite, individual preciousness to God, and at the same time to remain servants, because others need and are worthy of care. This is to follow Jesus, who did precisely this. Though he was the Son of God, he became a man, a carpenter, and served his Father's will. His Father's will was that Jesus serve us by pioneering a way for us. And Jesus recognized and received the Father's love as involving this service for us. We see in Mary this same combination: a recognition that elevation involves service to others. She bears the child, willing to face the scorn of doing so out of wedlock, and thereafter she undertakes all the mundane tasks of being a mother, without asking to be made a great lady with servants.

This combination of preciousness to God and service to others is a tremendous task. It is a task for a saint, yet it is one we are called to perform. Its difficulty should make us realize that the Christian life is not attained all at once, but in degrees and over a long period of time. It should not overwhelm us. For we obey our Father not as slaves but as children. That is, our services are performed in this world, often very mundane ones, as we are beset by the lure of material goods, security, prestige, and under the threat of all kinds of misfortunes and death. But we are not subject to these as slaves—at the mercy of where they carry us (whether to great fortune or destruction). Despite them we are moving to and into that reality where his love for us becomes clearer and more powerful. The heaviness of combining worth and concern is lightened by a trust that we are moving toward a mysterious goodness, which we are already beginning to experience.

We are of course tempted again and again to turn away from our elevation, and instead live in the human equation of superiority and inferiority. We keep finding ourselves unable to love people because we are so busy finding, lamenting, or glorifying our place in the standings.

It is for this reason that we need a society or community in which our worth is recognized right now. God's love reaches us with great effect if we are among others who have also known his love to some degree, and who together form a new society. It is a new or different society because its basis is Christ's way of service. The church is not and need not be a perfect community in order to be a place that helps us realize our own worth. It is really a meeting place of two worlds of values or two different standards. We are marked off from one another by the social standards of the day. Yet we recognize that such social standards are not a true measure of our worth because of God's love in Christ. All of us receive and give each other support in the struggle between these two standards. We give support when we receive *anyone*, regardless of social status, into the community who wishes to be part of Christ's new order; when we expose and lament the social captivity under which we all still labor; when, even in the simplest acts, we transcend those gaps between us created by social prestige. We do it even when we exchange a friendly word with each other on the street.

This helps the one who is lowly in the world *and* the one who is high. It enables each to confess and manifest their solidarity that transcends all barriers. It gives a moment of relief to the ones who are lowly and feel each day the stigma of their station; it strengthens them to believe in their own worth and not to be overcome by the social standards of the day. To those with great social prestige, it gives a moment of truth. It pulls them out of the network of society and the false directions in which society pulls them. Each group helps the other. We need this constant contact with the church's society, in and outside the sanctuary. In it we receive our elevation from Christ by being freed of the social standards of this world. No matter how much prestige the world offers, it can never match the elevation we receive in the new reality we are called to enter.

All of us need help because we all pursue tasks and goals, some of them very worthwhile. When we do well, we feel good, and we should. But this can become a barrier between us and those who try and fail. Our achievement should have as its ultimate goal service or a gift to others. It should not be a means to elevate ourselves beyond all solidarity. Our private successes sometimes lead us to forget our solidarity with all people.

In like manner, those of us not so successful may have so little self-esteem that we feel no bond with anyone. We are cut off because we want to achieve and want to have the importance others have. Just to point us to Christ and to say, "He loves you" often is not effective in overcoming the terrible lack of self-love from which many of us suffer. It is also not to offer all that Christ expects and commands us to offer each other. We are literally to offer *sanctuary*— a society not founded, like the social system of worth, on the principles of self-expansion, chance, and force, but one whose maker and builder is God. For all its imperfections, the church is where *need* is recognized as the sole reason for concern and help. It is the place where we all turn together—with each other and for each other—to our Father, as we endure the scars, misfortunes, and humiliations of this life, and rejoice in our refusal to admit their authority and finality. We enjoy that mysterious reality that envelops us whenever we reach out to each other and with each other for our Father.

What we are to be is indeed still hid in God. That is, our elevation is complete only when the kingdom comes in fullness. At present, our awareness of the kingdom and therefore of ourselves is fleeting, appearing and disappearing from our view as our present imperfections temporarily obscure it. One day we shall live and move and have our being in its reality, without shadow and interruption. But we begin to receive what we are to be now, as together, as a society, as a people, we wrestle out of what we now are, into what we will be.

It should be recognized, however, that the degree to which we succeed in finding effective relief is often largely beyond our control. For example, a person may be abandoned by a spouse after years of marriage. This person may have always been a person with low self-esteem anyway, and the abandonment adds a crushing confirmation to this low estimate of worth. Another person may have wanted to marry but for some reason or other never found anyone. A young person may have certain physical characteristics associated with the opposite sex, and suffers terribly at the torments inflicted on him by peers in high school. Theoretically much can be done to help all three of these people. However, in practice quite often not enough is done or can be done, given a particular town, school, or church, to enable such people to find what would be considered a fairly satisfying life. Pointing them to or reminding them of Christ's love may help them bear some of the pain and humiliation. Compassionate concern by those in the church can provide some relief. But social unacceptability is a powerful force, and it exacts a heavy toll that we cannot always sufficiently mitigate.

Certain agencies offer various kinds of therapy to help people whose self-worth is being battered by society, and they do provide a great service. But they are limited in what they can do to help us find our true worth. Sometimes they only enable us to become socially successful. To free us of the suffering caused by social unacceptability is certainly a good thing. But to be socially acceptable does not give us an accurate measure of our true worth. It may not in the least enable us to have compassion for others, or to realize how much of a role chance plays in determining the status we all have. A sense of solidarity, which is one sign that we are beginning to find our true worth, may be totally absent in us though we now "feel good" about ourselves.

To desire to feel good about ourselves can even get in our way. To aim for it *directly* may cut us off from others. We can be so conscious of ourselves and how we feel that we do not really pay attention to other people. The final goal of life is not to feel good about myself. It is to be in communion with others. Then we indeed do feel good about ourselves, but this has occurred *indirectly*. We have joy because we are enjoying the presence of others, and they are enjoying us. This is perhaps what Jesus meant when he said, "Do not let your left hand know what your right hand is doing" (Matt. 6:3).

I personally used to be nervous when addressing people because I was very worried about what they would think of me. But whenever my goal becomes to make every effort to convey to them *what* I am talking about because I think it will matter to them, I worry much less. The goal of the talk becomes what *they* will get out of it. Failures still occur, but it is a very different matter to be disappointed because some people did not receive something that I thought would be of value to them. The focus of my disappointment is thus not so much what they thought of me. Success is different too. The expressions of gratitude do not become a temptation to pride. In expressions of gratitude I am receiving another person; I am receiving persons who now enjoy what I wanted them to have. So we have a common joy, and *that* makes me feel good. The common decency of paying attention to other people's welfare is not a new idea. It is something we all know about. That is true not simply of this step along the way but of all the arches of the gateway. Our restlessness, which material goods cannot still, our vulnerability to harm, the inaccuracy of the social gauge of importance, are not new ideas. Yet we may not have seen their spiritual significance. We may not have allowed them to start shaping our lives, or the direction of our lives. Simply as facts known to us, they are prosaic and useless. But seen as truths that mark out a path to God, their significance may start to dawn. They begin to ferment and grow as they shape our attitudes, our outlook, our actions—as I just illustrated most simply in my own case of making addresses to people. They then start to open us to a new world. They enable us to realize that in these ordinary things we are able to start living in quite specific ways in God's presence. They enable us to receive nourishment from God. Each part of this pilgrimage is ordinary; its novelty consists in where it leads us and what we receive as we walk.

To receive the elevation God offers us in Christ is to start moving into community—to allow a bond created by his love of us in Christ to develop between us. That bond resists separation caused by our social system, and reinforces the bond we recognize by our common exposure to upheaval. It enables us to find joy in each other. This is what it is to be lowly, to be humble: not to *feel* lowly, but to find joy in others. As we turn to each other we begin to find our true value and identity; and our identity ultimately culminates in a community with God and with each other that is free of imperfections and tenuousness. "Blessed are the poor in spirit, for theirs is the kingdom of heaven" (Matt. 5:3).

five

THE MONOTONY
OF WORK

The transformation of our activities from self-aggrandizement to service, as we have seen, is one of the marks of our openness to the elevating love of God. One of our most time-consuming, important, and necessary activities is our work. From it we derive not only our living but much of our significance and worth. The connection between work and self-worth is so strong throughout life that we can see its effects even in retired people. Some people upon retirement have to struggle with the feeling that they are now back numbers, and have trouble maintaining their own sense of dignity. The women's movement is in part a demand to be allowed to enter any occupation because inferior jobs and inferior pay are so closely connected with inferior status.

Since work and worth are so deeply related, the next step along the way has to do with work. How does our work enhance or hinder our ability to receive the love of God? How does it encourage or retard our development of humility? How may it help our true identity to emerge?

Not every aspect of these questions can be explored here. Only those matters that show us the next step in our pilgrimage are relevant. These can be uncovered by a study of the Christmas story, in particular the visit of the shepherds and wise men to Bethlehem. The story is so associated with childhood that we may fail to see that it reveals truths that are not childish, but full of wisdom. Sometimes it is the very places where God shows himself most clearly that we find it most difficult to perceive his presence. So let us look closely at the story of the visit of the shepherds and wise men for what it may teach us about our work and how our work can help or hinder us from moving deeper into God's love.

Let us begin with the apparently trivial fact that the wise men were late. They did not get to Bethlehem on the night of Jesus' birth. According to the story, they missed the glory of hearing the angels' song and learning from it that they were to go to Bethlehem immediately. It was the shepherds who had that privilege. They found the Christ child first and offered him their worship. The wise men came along some days later.

This time difference may reflect a difference between two types of people: intellectuals and laborers. There are many other types of people than these two, but let us look at these two, since their work will reveal some things that are true of all kinds of work.

The wise men, intellectuals of their day, were students of the stars. As astronomers, they used the very advanced mathematics and observational skills developed over hundreds of years in Babylon, and so were wise even by present-day standards. Astronomers were very important because it was believed that human destiny was connected with the stars. By studying the stars people got valuable information about what was to happen. So a king would consult star-gazers about future trends, just as our rulers nowadays consult professors of economics and sociology.

The wise men then were intellectuals—those who had whatever knowledge there was to be had.

The early Christian church was proud of the fact that the wisdom of the East—represented in the wise men— recognized the superiority of Christ. Their wisdom led them to seek Christ and to worship him.

But, as I have said, the wise men of the East were a little late. The shepherds got there first: not the intellectuals but the laborers. Why? Why did God send angels to laborers and reveal to them where Christ lay, whereas wise men had to follow a star and make a great journey to get there? I think perhaps it means that those who labor are closer to the realities of life. They are closer to the truth of our human condition; for what is labor in essence? It is monotonous; it is repetitive; it is the same old thing over and over. It wears your body out. You can become so weary that your mind is filled only with your aches and pains and every other thought is driven out. When it is unremitting and cruel, labor reduces us to a lump of matter, to the very clay out of which we are formed. The shepherd's life was not that hard but it was a laborer's life. It was lonely; it was monotonous. The same round year after year of lambing, protecting, finding pasture, disease, strays, shearing, market; the same thing over and over again.

An intellectual constantly has novelty: new ideas, new discoveries, new books to read, new specimens to examine—an endless task but an ever new one, with plenty of variety to occupy the mind.

But the shepherd—the one who labors—is closer to the truth than those who spend their lives seeking truth. For labor by its monotony, by its repetition, by its boredom can teach us what it is to be a human being *without* God. It can teach us that we are hungry for something more than we have, hungry for more than anything the world has or can give. Laborers are closer to this truth and have it ground into their very bodies and minds. The very restrictions of their circumscribed lives can teach them that work is not where we find our true worth; for it does not fill a person. We have capacities that it does not satisfy. Here again we see in operation the law: from suffering can come understanding.

The intellectual is kept from this truth, from what it is to be without God, for a long time. His life is constantly filled with variety; his work is interesting; it is constantly sweetened by the prospect of reputation or even fame. He is part of a long line of noble research that has added immeasurably to our store of knowledge and power. He is frequently shown deference and respect. The hunger for more than this world can give is kept in check by these tidbits. He does not know what is in his own heart. But he can learn. In time the repetition is noticed: one group of students succeeds another until they are all pretty much the same. Idea after idea comes and goes; one sees so many ideas that in time it seems that there are not any more really new ones. Aristotle—nearly three hundred years before Christ—said there is nothing new under the sun. One hundred years before him the poet in Ecclesiastes said the same thing. Novelty ceases. Boredom comes later to intellectuals, but it comes. We hunger for more than we can find; and in time the intellectual can learn this. But those who labor in jobs that from the start lack variety learn it sooner.

So God is closer to shepherds than to wise men because their need for something truly worthwhile is a more pressing reality. Perhaps this is why the wise men were a little later getting to Bethlehem than the shepherds.

But the wise men did get there. The wisdom of the world—represented by these men—did recognize its need; for they came to worship the newborn king. They came to worship; not to see him, or to discuss or to talk about him. Their wisdom led them to a different kind of truth—to a person who is born to be king. He is a ruler who is good and because he is good he is *worth* being devoted to.

Because he is good he can take away evil; because he is loving, he can satisfy our hunger.

In the Old Testament the Queen of Sheba came to Solomon to test his wisdom and marveled at what he knew. The wise men came to a child who was king because he could fill the hunger of our hearts.

As the years went by the example of the wise men of the East was followed by the wisdom of Greece and Rome. The Christian religion became the religion of the best minds of the West. For centuries the greatest minds were devoted to Christ; they worshiped him. Their wisdom led to him, and he enhanced and completed their wisdom.

But what about our wisdom today? Where does it lead us? Does it lead us to Christ? Our universities in the West—the centers of learning—for the most part do not acknowledge Christ. In Princeton, where I live, it is interesting that the Theological Seminary and the University are separate institutions. The existence of the University Chapel is important. It shows that many *individuals* who are learned personally are Christians. That matters and is not to be dishonored in any way. Nonetheless it is also a fact that subject after subject, discipline after discipline, is not in any way informed by the wisdom of Christ. The pursuit of knowledge is not considered to be something that might lead to worship.

In fact, the word "wisdom" has been virtually discarded from our vocabulary of desirables in western society. The Greek word "philosophy" means love of wisdom. We instead honor *intelligence,* and there is a great difference between the two. Intelligence is a capacity for solving problems, for making discoveries, for bringing order out of confusion. But it is a limited capacity because it says nothing about applying what you learn to yourself. To say of someone that he is intelligent tells us nothing about his character; but to say of someone that he is wise does. We can see another difference by contrasting the effects of suffering on us. Suffering, as we have pointed out, can give us understanding or wisdom; but it cannot give us intelligence. Still another way to see that they are different is to notice that people can be wise who are not particularly intelligent; and people can be intelligent but not wise. The cross is said to be a place where the wisdom of God is made manifest (1 Cor. 1:18–2:12). The cross is a display of divine wisdom. Is it a wonder that a society that no longer seeks wisdom cannot perceive the significance of the cross? We will return to this a little further along in our pilgrimage.

If wisdom is not what is pursued in our universities, what is? What is our learning directed toward? What is it supposed to lead to? As we all know, much of it is directed toward helping people get good jobs. Some of it is directed toward bringing greater equality between people of different races and economic backgrounds. Some of it is directed to increasing our knowledge. Much of it is to produce teachers to succeed other teachers. But does it promise to give us or lead us to any truth that can satisfy the human heart and mind? My firm conviction is that nowadays university disciplines and intellectuals prefer to ignore that question. Every discipline—including philosophy, ethics, and sometimes religion—considers an actual earnest search for a deep meaning to life, every genuine search for personal fulfillment, to be outside its domain and in no significant way relevant to its procedures or results.

Our knowledge today, for all its genuine achievements, does not lead us anywhere. No one can study every subject or know all about a single subject. But from a lifetime of listening to others, I have hardly heard even a whisper in university academic activity of a truth or a good that can satisfy the heart and mind. Yet this fact is constantly ignored, passed over, as though a person who hungers for such truth were unbalanced or out of date. If our learning were more thorough, if it aimed at *wisdom* and not just learning, I think it would lead us as it did the wise men of old to recognize that all our treasures lack one great treasure: something or someone to love, and in that love to find wholeness and fullness of life.

All of us have to give of ourselves. We give our energy, our time, our emotions. Those who give themselves in work of physical or common labor often know that such an occupation is not worthy of their whole person. It is not worthy of their devotion. Such work never becomes an idol. And so laborers in their labor, precisely because it is so empty, are closer to the truth; for they are more easily aware of the fact that they have nothing. Those who are intellectuals can be deceived for a long time by thinking that what they work at is worthy of their attention; for it is more interesting than labor. But it is not worthy of their *full* attention either—however great and useful it may be. We are so made that nothing is good enough for us; nothing is worthy of our devotion. And we learn this—sooner or later—in the boredom of our work; this boredom cannot be fully hidden by the rewards of our work, no matter how various or legitimate. All people need to find something worthy of them. Laborers sometimes learn sooner than intellectuals that they need to seek.

One of the insights of labor is that our work cannot fulfill us. It takes humility to recognize this; for we have to learn that by our actions and efforts we cannot give ourselves fullness of life. If we are to find it, we will have to receive it. Workers are better placed to recognize this than intellectuals. This does not mean they are supposed to accept humiliating conditions. They have every right and reason to seek to improve their conditions of labor, and to find as much satisfaction in their work as possible. They have every right to find better work. They may do all this without losing the knowledge that no work, of whatever kind, can ever satisfy the hunger we all have for fullness of life. Of course efforts to improve our lot can get in the way of learning this truth. One can dream that a better job will bring happiness. But looking for a better job need not hide from us the truth that all work is limited in what it can do for us.

Its very limitations are an *indirect* revelation of our worth, of our preciousness; for they reveal to us our capacity for something greater than the satisfactions and status of work. To be able to perceive God's love is to be a creature of immense and remarkable capacity. That greatness can become real and concrete to us by the painful experience of work. We can actually *feel* our greatness in our suffering. The boredom, triviality, hardness, disappointment, anxiety, and precariousness of work—all of which are present to some degree in every kind of work—press the truth of our greatness into the very core of our being. They can make us experience bitterly how much we need to receive in order to be filled. From this very travail we can experience how much we are loved by God; for we suffer because he has made us for communion with him, and without it we are unfulfilled.

The great tragedy here, and indeed in so much of suffering, is that we suffer but we do not learn from it. We fail to distinguish how much of it is owing to oppression, to things that humiliate us and that ought therefore to be removed, and how much of it is from things that are unremovable and from which we can learn of our great destiny. It is not beyond the ability of any of us to think about our work. By thinking honestly about it, we can recognize how work does contribute toward our fulfillment, but realize that it cannot by itself be our fulfillment.

The boredom, disappointment, and anxiety we feel with our work can thus be transformed from a drag on our life into a step that leads us along the way to fullness of life. The suffering is real; but its very genuineness is what can drive us to look beyond where we now are to a *spiritual* reality to give us our hearts' desire. The hunger for that which nothing earthly can fill, when felt in the actual work we do, can change our work. It can enable us to see work as part of our apprenticeship as children of God, learning bit by bit what we need from our Father. There is then no shame in being a laborer, because there is no absolute barrier between the laborer and the intellectual or anyone else. All of us are in one sense engaged in the same work—finding out what it is we need from our Father, whether we realize it or not. As we learn more and more clearly that we have a spiritual hunger, we may ask him to feed us, and he will. He feeds those who are hungry for him, with his own presence. And I do not mean in esoteric or strange ways. To pray, to read or reflect on Scripture, to worship with fellow believers, to be with a believer, or even to reflect on the church in past ages—all can touch and nourish that mysterious emptiness at the very center of our person. The inspiration from God's life increasingly becomes our source of energy for living and acting.

six

OUR TALENTS

Our pilgrimage toward God has caused us to wrestle with three questions. What do I think of myself? What do other people think of me? What does God think of me? The answers often do not agree with each other. Within our own inner experience each of them is often felt as a violent pull in different directions. The way other people think of me is usually in terms of my social position—the house I live in, the car I drive, the job I hold, the status I have achieved in the community. But the way others think of me and treat me may be quite different from the way I feel about myself. Even if other people think of me as a success, my inner life may be a very painful one. I may be disappointed with what I am and what I have achieved. The divergence may be even more obvious with a person whose status is low but who thinks he is much more significant than the position he has. Nevertheless, this same disparity exists among the successful, even those with enormous prestige. Einstein was once quoted as saying he wished he had been a plumber. The way he said it made it clear that within himself he was a deeply disappointed person.

The way I think of myself may of course coincide with the way other people think of me. In fact, most of us probably move back and forth between an acceptance of the way other people think of us and a rejection of their opinions. But the way other people think of me is probably the way I think of myself most of the time, and on the most conscious level of my mind. Their view gives me an "objective" picture of what I am. A well-adjusted person is a person who can accept this objective picture. He can recognize the objective truth about what he is and who he is; he can accept and overcome the negative subjective feelings he has about himself that may be caused by the objective picture.

But we have reason to be skeptical about the accuracy of the way we are evaluated by others. The social status I have may be objective in the sense that it is indeed the way other people think of me. It may be objective in the sense that it truly reflects the place I hold in society—a janitor, a carpet salesworker, a preacher. Yet, as we have seen, our social position is based on a large element of chance, and it is subject to radical change by political and economic circumstances over which we frequently have no control. It cannot therefore be an accurate gauge of my true worth. So, even if I have come to terms with the way other people look at me, that does not mean I am aware of my *true* self.

This brings us to the third estimate of what I am— what God thinks of me. God's valuation does not correspond to what people think of me. It does not correspond to what I think of myself—whether I accept or reject other people's opinion of me. God does not encourage us to pretend that we do not have a social position or that it tells us nothing about ourselves. Nor does he ask us to ignore how we feel about our position. On the contrary, we are to be realistic about all this. We are to recognize in our inmost selves what others think of us, what our position in life is, and how we feel about it. Laborers and intellectuals, just to refer to two ways of life, should experience *fully* what it means to be what they are. To know and feel what you are in the society can be an opportunity. It can make you inwardly aware that whether you are high or low, there is something more that you need to be a truly full human being. You may not have the slightest idea what the need is, but you feel it and know it concretely. You feel it because you are realistic about your position in society, a position so heavily based on the work you do. In fact, you are *more* realistic than those who are merely well-adjusted, who have learned to accept themselves.

As we have taken each step in our pilgrimage, we have been learning a bit at a time what our true selves are. We have been uncovering step by step what it is that we are to be—the self that is hid with God—the person that we are to become because of his love. The next step we are to make asks us to continue to be realistic about ourselves. But this time it is to be realistic about our *talents*. We should ask what we think of ourselves as we look at our talents and achievements.

When we look at our talents and ask ourselves about our personal significance, we all know that we feel the agreement and disagreement, the currents and crosscurrents, of how other people think of us and how we think of ourselves. The pulls and tugs are known to us in our contrary feelings of self-pity and self-satisfaction, of anxiety and elation. In our next step we are going to try to feel the healing grace of God's estimation of us—to feel his love for us, as we think of our talents and our mixed feelings about them. We will see if we can experience the illumination God's love sheds on these counter pulls, and feel the joy and peace his love gives us as we think about our talents.

We will begin by thinking about a story Jesus once told. We have all heard his story about a rich man who, before he set out on a journey, entrusted his servants with "talents." A talent was a sum of money. In present-day English the word *talent* means ability, such as a talent for music or painting. In fact, this story of a rich man giving units of money called "talents" gave us our English word *talent* meaning capacities or abilities. So we can look at this story about money as a story also about capacities or talents.

One of the interesting things about the story is that the servants are not given equal talents. One has five talents, one has two, and the third servant has only one talent. The same thing is very true in life: people have different talents and some people are much more talented than others. We believe in democracy and equality of opportunity, but people are not equally endowed with talent. Some are much more intelligent, through no virtue of their own. Some are gifted musically; some are marvels at mathematics; others have fine voices. Others of us are very limited in our native endowments, again through no fault of our own.

Uneven distribution of talents is another of those conditions of life under which we live. We see in operation once again that spiritual law to the effect that we do not set the conditions or circumstances in which we are to find our fulfillment. Talents are very unevenly distributed, and we have nothing to do with our native endowment. It is by the way we *respond* to the fact of unevenness that we are to move closer or further away from the reality of God, further or closer to a discovery of our true self. For our true worth is not the same as our talents; our talents, though indeed valuable, are not an adequate measure of our worth.

Most of us are probably sometimes disappointed with the talents we have been given. We wish that we were more intelligent, or better looking, or taller or shorter. We seem always to run into someone who is more gifted than we are, and that sometimes gives us pain. Then too people who have talent get more attention than others. They usually are more interesting and achieve greater things than those who are more ordinary. This does not bother us all the time, but sometimes it makes us feel very bad.

There is indeed inequality in gifts, but there is a way in which we are equal. All of us are responsible; all of us have to face a judgment. According to the parable, the giver of the talents returns one day and calls the servants before him to see what they have done with their talents.

The idea of judgment is an awful one; it has a dreadful sound. You are put on the carpet and judged. You are measured, evaluated, sized up—and either praised or con-demned. We do not like the idea of judgment. Not even all the things we have done that we are proud of can make up for some of the other things we have done; they are bit-ter truths that mark our soul and fill us with regret. We wish there were no judgment; no judge who sees the truth.

And yet there is another side to the idea of judgment—an encouraging side. Judgment means that we are all taken with equal seriousness. All of us, whether we have great talents or just ordinary ones, matter enough to be judged. What we do with our talent is equally important; for it is not what we start with that counts. We have no responsi-bility for where we start; we are completely and perfectly innocent on that score. It is the *use* of our talents that matters, and here a just judgment is made. Those with five talents and those with two talents added the same amount to their natural endowment; each doubled what he began with and each was equally regarded. Each was equally praised, and each invited to the same banquet feast of the rich master. Presumably the servant with the one talent, had he doubled it, would have received the same treat-ment.

So a judgment, even though it is frightening, is also a way of saying that we are all equally important, equally regarded, equally significant. If there were no judgment, then we would not all count, and certainly not all count the same. Only those with great talent would have lives worthy of notice, lives to be taken seriously. The rest of us would be insignificant. But a judgment—a Lord who looks at each one of us to see what kind of life we have to offer—means that each of us has a life that matters, a life that is significant.

As one of my children's storybooks puts it, "A person's a person, no matter how small." The main classification is to be a *person*; differences in size do not affect the main classification. Differences in ability do not affect the main category in which we all stand.

We often feel sorry for the man in the parable who had only one talent. The man with five and the man with two were so much ahead of him. He seems a pretty small, incompetent creature. When he saw what the others had, he would have been justified in feeling, "What's the use. They have so much that they will do great things; who will notice me? I'm just a little person. I'll never amount to much." Self-pity can really get us down, especially when things go wrong.

Here again, to be more realistic and to know ourselves more truly we need a larger perspective. If you love mountains and take delight in the sublime feeling of their majesty, beauty, and power, then perhaps this comparison will help. Most of the earth's surface is not mountains. Only a few places on the earth soar upwards, so that when we stand on the plains they seem to rise up and nearly touch the sky. They completely dwarf us by their size and majesty. But as you know from photographs, if you get just a few miles out in space and can thus see the entire earth, all you notice is a round globe. There are no longer these great differences between mountains and plains. The great differences are lost from a greater perspective: all things in the world—mountains, plains, and seas—are seen together and appear truly wonderful and glorious. The first American in space, Alan Shepard, when his rocket reached its peak, looked down and saw the earth; and his first reaction was to gasp in wonder at its overwhelming beauty.

Most of us indeed are not very imposing when compared to people of great talent; they tower above us in ability like mountains above plains. And yet, the simple ability to talk—to use language, communicate with one another, something as common and ordinary as that, a talent nearly everywhere—that talent has never ceased to amaze the scientists and philosophers who study language. Language is such a complex and important talent that they are still struggling to explain how it is that we can talk. It is far more amazing that we can all talk than that some of us can talk better than others. The mountain of *beautiful* language indeed towers over the flat plains of *ordinary* language. But the very existence of language itself reduces the distance between them to the point where *both* seem to be an extraordinary talent.

All of us have more talent than we realize. We simply are so close to each other that we don't notice how remarkable each of us is; we are too close to great mountains to notice how they are simply peaks resting on a very remarkable earth. In the country of the blind, a man with eyes is king; where everyone has eyes, we forget how wonderful it is to see.

Jesus taught us that we are to employ our talent. Each of us in some particular way can do more good, bring more happiness, than anyone else in the entire creation. There are many, many things each of us cannot do and there is very much that is wrong. I cannot bring peace to the earth. I cannot bring justice. But I can bring enormous happiness and joy into the lives of my children today simply by noticing them, simply by taking time with them, simply by giving myself to them. No one else can do that for them, for it is me they want: *my* notice, *my* affection, *my* voice, *my* presence.

So it is with you: you are irreplaceable. Your irreplaceable gifts—your voice, your friendliness, your concern—are desired by someone. Only *you, only* you, can fill the bill. And Jesus is telling you: for God's sake do not bury your talent. In his kingdom it is not how much you have, but the *use* you make of what you have and are that counts. So even though the idea of judgment is distasteful, the parable of the talents really ought to encourage us. It tells us that the life of each one of us matters. We do not all have equal talents, but we all do have talents, and we are all—great or small—important. The life of each of us is noticed by God; and God *expects* each of us to serve and to employ our talents to the full.

The use of our talents has another spiritually important value. The only way we can begin to find out who we are, and what the world we live in is like, is by use of our talents. The only way we can discover our internal limitations and the limitations of our surroundings is to employ and develop our abilities. Those who do not use their talents, who bury them, by this failure to act fail to learn what is and what is not possible. It is only by an attempt to develop our potential and to express our talents that we can move forward in our pilgrimage. It is the only way to develop humility; the only way to learn how much of us is a false self; the only way to get into a shape that can receive the life God seeks to give us. To withhold ourselves, to bury ourselves, is not humility. We do not renounce ourselves by burying ourselves. We become humble through an exercise and expression of ourselves. It is by striving to achieve that we can ask ourselves, What is it I am trying to do? What am I after? Am I really giving any serious thought to doing anything for other people in the *main* activities I pursue? If we never try to achieve anything, how can we get into the position of asking ourselves such questions?

There was a man I once knew who became principal of a school. The organization under his leadership prospered. The budget was balanced. Much better administrative procedures were developed. But he felt sometimes that some people resented him. He wasn't sure. It was just a vague sort of feeling he sometimes got. After a while teachers' morale noticeably declined; some teachers transferred to another school. Why? He had always been polite, thoughtful, considerate. He had always tried to do what was best for the school. What had gone wrong? When we are in a similar position ourselves, if we are honest and keep on asking ourselves and listening to thoughtful advice, we may find out. We may learn, as this man did, that we do not always give other people a chance to express themselves. We do not give them enough scope to use *their* talents. If we can accept this, we gain the chance to learn what it is voluntarily to restrict ourselves. We learn to shape our desires so as to make room for other people's legitimate aspirations. We have the chance to learn to be humble. We would never have had such a chance if we had not accepted the initial challenge to use our talents.

By trying, we succeed or fail in our ventures. Our reactions to success or failure are places where we can grow. We can ask ourselves how we feel about our successes and failures. Does failure in a venture really mean we are a failure? Does success really mean we are a success? What are successes and failures anyway? Only if we try to use our talents do the discrepancies and agreements between how I feel about myself, what others think of me, and what God thinks of me fruitfully arise. The thoughts and feelings provided by these questions allow us to move forward.

Are you beginning to learn from your attempts to find a full and happy life that you are like a half-filled glass, which in spite of all you gain and put into it, gets no further to the top because there is a hole in the bottom? How could you learn this if you never tried to find fullness of life?

Thus it is through a use of our talents, not by neglecting them, that we have the *opportunity* to become humble. We can learn in time to use our talents for the benefit of others; we can learn how voluntarily to limit our self-expression so that other people can use their talents as well; we can learn how empty we are at the very center of ourselves, however much we have. We learn for ourselves the truth of Jesus' words, "To him who has will more be given; and from him who has not, even what he has will be taken away" (Mark 4:25).

The word *opportunity* is very important. A weakness in the popular clamor today for self-expression and realization of one's potential is that these are treated as *final goals*, as stopping points. Self-expression and development of one's talents are not seen as a *step* in a journey. Can I find fullness of life in the social prestige my self-expression brings? Can I find fullness of life simply in my internal satisfaction over what I have done, apart from what others think of me? The struggle we feel even when we fulfill our potential is itself a strong reason to think we have not reached our final goal.

We do not always feel insignificant when we look at our talents and achievements. Ironically, we sometimes feel just the opposite; we feel self-sufficient. We often think of ourselves as standing on our own feet. We take our talents and natural endowments for granted. Although we had nothing to do with it, we tend to feel that our natural endowment is ours: our brains, our strength, our looks. But God looks at us differently. We are in fact responsible for only one aspect of our talents— their *use* or *misuse*. They are ours to employ. But we are not completely independent; we are not self-sufficient.

But have we learned to see what we have as a gift? Does gratitude form part of our character, so that gratitude is part of our basic outlook, deeply affecting our behavior? This is part of the step we are now making—becoming grateful. Unless we have become grateful, we have not really *received* our talents. We have *taken* what has been given. We have made them our own without any acknowledgment of a giver. So we are closed to the giver's reality; we are not able to receive even more, because we have never really received from him what we now have. We lack humility—a realistic assessment of ourselves. We have assumed, and been confirmed by the society around us in our assumption, that we stand on our own feet and make progress by our own efforts alone.

This common and deeply held attitude is perhaps what lies behind a very unusual episode in Jesus' life. Once when hungry, Jesus went to a fig tree seeking fruit. But it was bare because it was not the season for fruit. He cursed it: "May no one ever eat fruit from you again" (Mark 11:14). He then visited the Temple, and cast out the moneychangers. Upon leaving the Temple he went past the fig tree, and the disciples noticed that it had withered.

It seems strange indeed to curse a tree for having no fruit when it is the wrong time of year for fruit. It may seem that Jesus had lost his temper and abused his powers. Actually the episode may mean that none of us can bear fruit *by ourselves*. Only God is the source of good and by his secret and untraceable actions comes every good and perfect gift. We indeed receive these gifts. They become our own, and we can pass good on to others. By giving we join God's graciousness as one who gives. But ultimately all good things have their source in God. They have a giver who must continually be acknowledged; otherwise *in time* we become barren. Over a period of time our attitude of self-sufficiency cuts us off from the source of goodness. We may grow leaves, but we will not bear fruit; that is, what we have will not produce good.

It has taken me years in the ministry to begin to learn how true this is. My natural endowments are better than average. My upbringing made me hard-working, determined, and ambitious. As I grew up, I received a great deal from people outside my home, especially my church, so that I developed a decent character and a concern for people. So when I began my ministry, I found I could do an awful lot *by my own efforts*. In fact, if I had not made the effort, the church I served would have collapsed. I was thoroughly aware of this—so much so that I felt a bit hypocritical sometimes when I prayed for God's help for myself or others, or listened to other people pray for it. I knew that praying for God's assistance helped *psychologically*. But the very knowledge that it was by *my* efforts that things were getting done quietly and slowly eroded my earlier simple faith.

This showed itself in the way my congregation became a burden to me: How was I ever to communicate to them all the great truths of the Christian faith? How was I ever to get them to be what they ought to be? Their failures, their weaknesses, their stubbornness, their sins, and their worldliness were tremendous weights that increasingly pressed me down. Some years later when I became a teacher, it was the same—struggling to help prepare young men and women for the ministry. What a burden improving people had become.

What I had received from God had become used up. The inspiration of God, the good I had received from him by natural endowment, from my prayers, and the influence of other people who bore his Spirit, was running dry. I experienced this in the discouragement I felt in trying to help other people. I experienced it in my resentment of other people's achievements; the prickle of envy I felt when others were praised for their ministry, when I felt I had done as much or more and I was not getting the credit I deserved.

No external crises ever occurred. In fact, I was generally successful in my churches and wherever I taught. But without realizing it, in the burden and discouragement and envy I felt, I was learning what it is to lose the sustaining goodness of God. I was learning what it is to try to be self-sufficient; to learn what it is to be cut off from the source and to live off my capital. It takes a long time to use up your capital, years in some cases. But in the ways I have described, I began to feel, to experience, to have rubbed into my every thought and action, that I was not self-sufficient.

I have learned from this once again to thank God for every lovely and beautiful human action, to be moved by

the goodness I see in other people. For I am now beginning to realize once again that it is indeed from him that
everything good ultimately comes. To be independent—
not intentionally but without even realizing it—has
taught me how true it is that we have a giver. To live without gratitude and dependence on him is eventually to lose
the renewing power of his Spirit. We dry up. We can no
longer work with joy. We sense no thanksgiving for what
others have and for what we have. Now I no longer find it
a burden to try to help others be in contact with God's
presence. People do not weigh heavily on me for *that* reason. (They do sometimes for other reasons.) I now quite
often get an enormous lift when someone seems to gain
something of value from my efforts; now I know that if
they have received anything of genuine value or goodness,
it is from their contact with the Father. I work just as hard
as ever, but I know that whatever spiritual good comes of
it, comes from him. I am not free of all anxiety or desire
for reputation; but I am beginning to realize that whatever is worth being proud of comes from God, however much
my efforts help open people to his presence. All I can do,
all I am asked to do, is to help people receive, receive from
him.

The fig tree is a parable of self-sufficiency. A fig tree
produces fruit in season by its own nature—or so it seems.
It seems to be able to yield fruit by the natural course of
events, apart from God. But Jesus went to it out of season,
found no fruit, and cursed it. It is as though it could have
had fruit even out of season had it relied on God; for to
produce in season or out of season is really a power given
by God. To produce in season is no more independent of
God than to produce out of season. To forget this is to
become cursed and barren, unable to produce fruit even in
season. Going to the tree out of season when its limitations were obvious, Jesus made the point that it could not
bear even in season without God's power. It is cursed for
its self-sufficiency.

All of us who forget that what we have is a gift, who try to produce out of our own self-sufficiency, become cursed with barrenness sooner or later. Even what we can do "naturally" by our own power ceases to do good. "From him who has not, even what he has will be taken away."

The grounds for this interpretation is the order of events. In Mark Jesus visits the tree, looks for fruit, then curses it. Immediately he goes to the Temple, finds moneychangers there and drives them out with the words, "Is it not written, 'My house shall be a house of prayer for all the nations'? But you have made it a den of robbers" (Mark 11:17). The next event is Peter's exclamation, as they pass the fig tree, "Master, look! The fig tree which you cursed has withered" (Mark 11:21b). Jesus answers with an encouragement to have faith in God, in particular to pray with confidence that we will receive.

The episode of the fig tree straddles the event in the Temple. This suggests that we are to understand these two events in relation to each other, especially as the Temple is called a house of prayer and Jesus speaks of prayer in connection with the withered fig tree. Jesus believes that Israel had corrupted its relationship with God. They had been called to be a special people, with the gift of a unique knowledge of God and a unique destiny. Their Temple was the place where dependence on God was visibly expressed. Here prayers were to be offered to God: prayers of thanksgiving for what they had received, prayers and sacrifices for forgiveness, and prayers for help and guidance. But the place where dependence was to be expressed had changed from a house of prayer to a place controlled by the priests. It had become a place of profit, and in one extreme case, moneychanging, a shady business. The place where people are to ask for help was turned into a place where people had become robbers, taking from God, not asking. The Temple, like the fig tree, no longer bore fruit because it had lost its dependence on God. It was making a go of things on its own.

When we go it on our own, taking what we have already received as our own without a deep sense of gratitude, and without asking again and again for more help, we become robbers. When we produce only in season, out of ourselves without reference to him as the source, we in time cease to be agents of that secret and mysterious goodness that can come only from him. We become barren. Our church and our individual lives, though successful in any number of ways, are less and less agents of his graciousness. They begin to wither when disconnected from the vine. We bear his name; we call on his name; we work in his name. But we do not have that life within us that gives life. So we bear no fruit for others to eat. Like the fig tree that was cursed, we have only leaves. Such leaves remind us of the leaves Adam and Eve used to cover their shameful nakedness after they had asserted their independence. Our activities produce many things but not spiritual good; they only cover up our inability to produce good, a good that nourishes the emptiness at the center of people.

Whatever we have must continually be renewed by that invisible power that keeps us from becoming robbers and finally barren; for only God is good, and he must renew his gifts or they in time cease to bear good fruit. All this is the result of having been made by a Creator, a Creator who seeks to have us live in communion with him. We become progressively less as we live outside of that communion, because it is by offering ourselves back to him from which all has come that we are open to becoming more. We enter more deeply into that communion that keeps building us up, transforming us more nearly into that which we are yet to become. We need to *ask*, constantly to ask, if we are to receive.

Most of us seem to have to learn this the hard way. Our ability is so obvious, our efforts so concrete, so indispensable, that an invisible reality on whom we are supposed to depend seems in comparison to be only a theory. Only when we find ourselves failing, with things getting out of control and going awry, do we remember that there is supposed to be a God. We then turn to him and ask for help.

But this may be only for help to get us what we have set out to get for ourselves. There is no change in our goals, no repentance about our direction. This is to try to use God as a means to get our ends. Such a turning is not to renounce our robbery, but an attempt to continue it. To call on God's name—even if it is accompanied by terrible suffering, inner turmoil, and genuine fear—is not automatically to get help. It may take a lot of such asking— with no answer, with no help—before we finally can say, "All right, you're in charge. What am I supposed to do? What direction am I supposed to walk in? What am I to do with myself?" So many of us seem to have to learn the hard way—if we learn at all—that we have taken what we have for granted.

Jesus died between two thieves—people who took as their own what was not theirs. One of them railed at Jesus, saying, "Are you not the Christ? Save yourself and us!" (Luke 23:39b). Get us out of the jam our robbery has led us to. But the other thief repented. He told the one who scoffed, "We are receiving the due reward of our deeds" (Luke 23:41), and then he asked Jesus, "Jesus, remember me when you come into your kingly power" (Luke 23:42). He was a realist. He knew he was a thief; but he now recognized to whom he belonged. The other thief was a "realist" too. He lived as a thief, and he died as a thief. His opinion of himself was perfectly in tune with what others thought of him. He had the courage to say so. He was a perfectly adjusted human being.

God's view is different. He knows we cannot find fullness of life out of our own resources. To those who have learned this, like the repentant thief, or less dramatically and painfully, like me, God can and does give. He gives his very own self, a communion with his mysterious presence that even now begins to enable us to feel, in his love for us, what we are to become.

seven

COMMITMENT

O ur talents and our work, our possessions and our
ambitions greatly affect our happiness, as we have
seen. But perhaps nothing affects it more in a day-to-day
way than the quality of our family life and our friendships.
Anthony Trollope in his novel *Barchester Towers* has an
amusing vignette about a bishop. The bishop is very ambitious and successful, but he is henpecked. One day, fed up,
he rebels against his wife, and immediately feels the satisfaction of being at last master in his home. But the sweet
taste of victory soon turns bitter. His wife finds a thousand
and one ways to make his homelife a misery. The dinner is
not properly cooked; his clothes are not back from the
laundry; he cannot sit quietly smoking his pipe in his
favorite chair without silly interruptions. She wins the
battle.

Family life and friendship have many ingredients.
There is, however, only one of them that forms the next
step along our way. It is commitment. Without commitment to other people we have neither friends nor a family. Commitments establish a connection between ourselves and others. As we will see in this step, it is only by
commitments that we can truly learn to know another

person, and indeed to be truly known ourselves. Our own genuine worth is hidden from others and even from ourselves until we make commitments.

Commitment highlights an ingredient of every journey—namely, time. It takes time to make a journey, especially the spiritual journey we are making. And time is involved in commitments. Precisely how we will now explore.

We all know that we cannot do very many things at the same time. When too many demands are put on us we exclaim, "I can only do one thing at a time!" We are, however, able to feel more than one way at a time; ambivalent feelings of love and hatred, of pride and self-pity can be present at the same time. Still, a moment of time can hold only so much. It cannot contain the entire range of human feelings at once any more than we can do everything at one time.

But because there are many different times, we can do one thing at one time and another at another time. As it is put in Ecclesiastes, we can weep at one time, laugh at another; mourn one day, and dance on another; keep and cast away; speak and be silent; love and hate; plant and harvest. There are many activities, moods, attitudes, and emotions that we could not have unless there were time—different times—so we could do, feel, and be different things. We can put ourselves fully into a game, forgetting all else, and then at another time attend to a child as if that child were the whole world. Then at another time we can be engrossed in a difficult problem at work or absorbed in a novel. We are creatures of time, able to be completely absorbed in one moment and then to live quite differently in another moment.

But can we *give* ourselves in a moment? Can we gather our entire selves up in one moment of time and commit ourselves fully, completely, and sincerely for the *rest* of time? Jesus called us to commit ourselves to him—to follow him, to be devoted to him, because he leads us to the

Father. Our whole pilgrimage presupposes that we can make commitments. But can we? Can we make such a commitment?

The same question faces us in our everyday life with other people. We are supposed to devote ourselves in marriage to another person for better or for worse, in sickness and in health, for richer or for poorer, until death. Parents are committed to children and children to parents. Commitments extend beyond one moment. Can we at one moment give ourselves, commit ourselves fully and completely beyond that moment and in some cases commit ourselves for all time?

This question may never have occurred to us. Our immediate attention is often occupied by a series of momentary attractions, such as a ballgame, a party, or a new outfit. On the horizon the expectation of something new and exciting, such as a trip abroad, a new house, a promotion fill up our minds. We easily drift along from one moment to the next, so that our lives become a series of bits and pieces without anything substantial running through them and connecting the pieces together.

Can we lead a thoughtless life, going from one thing to the next, and also have genuine friendships and a marriage? To find out what another person is really like, and for another truly to know us, takes time. It cannot be done by living a series of unconnected moments. We have to commit ourselves to rearranging our lives to have time for each other. Afterwards, as we learn to know each other, we start to recognize each other's needs. Genuine friendship or marriage implies a commitment to help each other. Only when we show such concern can we receive gratitude; only by loyalty to another can such gratitude be awakened in another person. So although commitments oblige and restrict us, they are an opportunity for deeper levels of human relations to be achieved. Thoughtless people think we can know and be known without being tied down, restricted, obligated. They think we can do just as we feel from moment to moment without missing anything. To the thoughtless person, commitments are like a ball and chain. But if we avoid the obligations placed on us by commitments, the opportunity truly to know another person and to be known by another is lost.

We cannot, then, lead a thoughtless life and have genuine friendship or a marriage. We have to have enough interest and concern for another person to make the sacrifices a commitment requires. But does not the idea of a lifelong commitment to another person still seem, at least sometimes, like a restriction, like a ball and chain, especially the idea of lifelong marriage? Have we really got the ability nowadays to make such commitments and to find them fulfilling?

Quite frankly, nowadays we are not very well equipped for genuine friendship or marriage. Material progress, so beneficial in many cases, has sheltered us from hardship at the price of putting us out of touch with so much of the real world. The unprecedented wealth of industrial countries bathes us in the heady aura of continuous supplies of goods and pleasures—as long as we find the money. We have no deep grasp of the connection between ourselves and our environment. Few of us, for example, watch the weather with our very lives at stake because a bad harvest means death. We simply do some work for some money, shove the money into a system we do not comprehend, and lo and behold there are the goodies. Our most common limitation is money. Even here the connection between work for which we are paid and serving an essential need by our work is not always apparent or even very strong. It often does not even exist.

So we do not get very much practice at learning what is real. We have no firmly fixed boundaries whose very immobility gives us reference points around which to locate ourselves. Without bumping into limitations, without the humility that comes from having our overextended self knocked back, we have no shape. We develop little character. We are so unpracticed at dealing with the real world that when it does break through in the form of children, illness, old age, and death, we are poorly prepared for them. When we run into real boundaries and limitations that call for a re-ordering of our lives, we flounder and do not profit from the opportunity they give us to find out who and what we are.

Limitations are an opportunity for us to learn to be realistic, to become humble. Without humility, without the ability to control our wishes and desires, we are not well-suited to live fruitfully with other people. We do not have the self-discipline or the character to make the sacrifices of time and selfish wishes it takes to stick with another person. We lack the strength to meet a commitment. We thus lose the opportunity really to know people, really to have a friend or a marriage. We never know loyalty and devotion, generosity and gratitude, support through trial, or the joy of being wanted. Whenever any real effort is required of us, whenever we need to make a deep adjustment that will allow a relationship to continue, we are tempted to give up and move on to someone else, because we lack the strength to face the challenge.

The sheltered lives we lead encourage us to become thoughtless. We are encouraged to flit from moment to moment, activity to activity, possession to possession, person to person. The beauty to be found only through commitment is thus inaccessible to us. In fact, we are increasingly told today that commitment is not beautiful. It is said, for example, that lifelong commitment in marriage is an arbitrary holdover from a bygone religious age. Actually, whatever marriage may be, it is not arbitrary. Its foundations are in the depths of our own person; it is in that deep longing genuinely to know another person and truly to be known ourselves. To hedge on our commitment to another is really to hedge on how much we think they are worth.

It takes time to discover worth. Its full depths are not apparent from the start. We have to venture, to act with faith that there is more than we have seen so far. A genuine marriage is a pledge of faith that we love enough to go into the future, with the confidence that another person is worthy of our lifelong devotion. It is also the humble reception of another person's faith in our being worthy of his or her lifelong devotion.

But what about Christ's call for commitment to him? Can we nowadays give ourselves fully and completely to him? Can we find in him the strength to fulfill our commitments to our family and friends, and find a deeper joy in them?

One of Jesus' greatest disciples, Peter, had trouble following his Lord. Yet he became a rock. Can we, like Peter, find the strength to have a life that holds together, that is more than a series of momentary bits and pieces? Let us see what made it hard for Peter to remain firm, and how he overcame his difficulties. Let us see if we can learn from him how to find a deeper and truer life by staying on the path Jesus pioneered for us. Let us see if we can become greater people through this commitment. Let us see how by the discipline of a great commitment we can become empowered to live fruitfully with other people, and find greater joy in friendship and marriage.

Peter is portrayed in the New Testament as a decisive person. He could size up a situation, bring himself to a focus, and commit himself then and there. He left his father by the sea when he was called by Jesus. Later when Jesus asked the disciples, "Who do you say that I am?", it was Peter who answered by confessing that Jesus was the Christ. Still later when Jesus washed the disciples' feet, it was Peter who resisted and said that he would not allow the Lord to wash his feet. It was Peter who pledged with all his might that he was ready to go to prison and even to death with his Lord. In each of these moments, Peter tried to give himself fully and completely, without reservation.

Yet we find that no sooner had he recognized the Christ than he was severely rebuked for uttering words that put him on Satan's side. Despite his vow to the contrary, his feet were washed by the Lord. After his last pledge of loyalty he denied Jesus three times before the next dawn.

What was wrong with Peter? Is it true that he was impulsive, ready to go off half-cocked, a lovable but foolish man? My view is that he was instead a person who wanted terribly to do what was right, and who had such purity of heart that he could will one thing: to devote himself to the glory he saw revealed in Jesus. Instead of a person we can feel superior to and think of in a patronizing way, Peter is one whose ability to pull himself together, his whole self, and to give himself mind, body, and soul, forever and ever to his Lord, judges us. No wonder the disciples regarded him as their leader; he did lead.

How is it then that he kept failing? If he really did give himself fully, completely, wholly, and sincerely, why the rebukes? why the vacillation? why finally outright denial? Peter was not in control of all that he was; nor was he in control of all the events that began to unfold and that would reveal to him and to others all that he was. There were desires, hopes, fears, and aspirations he did not realize he had. Above all he did not yet know the power of that tenacious, unreflective, untaught self-concern that goes by the name of egotism. He was sincere in his confession, in his commitment, in his vows and professions. All that he could muster was put into them; those moments contained all of himself that he could put into them. But there was more than he had control over, more to him than he knew, more to him than could be gathered up and given to his Lord in any single moment. He could not give himself in one moment, though he tried to and wanted to.

He needed time. He needed things to happen to reveal more of what he was, to reveal hidden aspirations, desires, hates, and fears. He needed more than one or two moments before the ruthless power of self-concern could become more evident to him. The same is true of us. We, like him, need a loving Lord who asks us more than once whether we love him, and who does not turn away from us when we fail. We need someone who sticks with us as we try but fail to stick with him.

But we often have not fully realized what Peter learned. We are tempted to think that we can give ourselves fully in a moment. One way we fall into this is by thinking that there is some turning point in our lives when we become committed to God, so that we put all our past behind us, and henceforth we are basically, primarily, and essentially good. Some of us cling to the moment of repentance, which was indeed in my own case a thrilling, wonderful, and never-to-be-forgotten moment. But it is also a temptation: for it is tempting to think that in that moment all that is evil has been cast away, and henceforth we never really deviate from our commitment.

Seven men burned a black man to death a few years ago in Mississippi. They all believed in Jesus Christ as their Lord and Savior. Apparently his Lordship did not extend very far. An extreme example? Indeed it is. So was Peter's denial. So is our denial of the fact that our person is not fully under our control and cannot be *given*, totally and wholly, to anyone or anything in a moment, however beautiful and thrilling a moment it may be. We need more than a moment to become committed and devoted.

Another temptation of the moment is sexual promiscuity and the way it is rationalized. It is sometimes justified on the ground that people really do give of themselves in such cases. They passionately and truly do love each other, and so it is all right, even good. The *quality* of the relationship is stressed in contrast to the *quantity* of enduring commitments, suggesting that quality makes up for duration. But can you really give yourself in a moment? The same considerations that applied to Peter apply here; and indeed an additional consideration applies here.

Simon Peter *tried* to give himself. The proof of that was that he intended and attempted to give himself for *all time*. The intensity or sincerity of our giving is tested by time; longevity is one test of sincerity, one test of good and evil intentions. A person who "gives" himself for the moment, who "gives" of himself for as long as he feels like it, has not given *himself* at all; has not even *tried* to give himself.

Love and devotion of the kind with which we are called to follow Jesus, with which we are to love one another so as to become one flesh, with which we are to be devoted as parents to children and children to parents, is love in which we give *ourselves*. Such a gift goes beyond any moment or moments, and its sincerity is that it is given without any time conditions. Intensity of passion, the "felt sincerity" of the moment, are not a sufficient indication of love; time and our intention concerning time reveal whether we love. They reveal the magnitude of our love, and the kind of love we give. They test whether we are seeking to give *ourselves*, and whether another desires to receive *us*. Community is a costly business because in order to receive another we must give ourselves. Such renunciation is an act of humility, but we can receive another only that way.

Shall we then say that since we cannot give ourselves in a moment, it is silly to commit ourselves? And if there are no commitments, but an open-eyed no-strings-attached mutual understanding, may we not do as we like with one another? That's folly! That would be to throw our lives away; to squander our lives in a series of moments, none of which contains us, all of which together do not add up to us because they do not add up to a complete person. We need time, and the only way we get time, in contrast to a series of unconnected moments, is through commitments. Commitments create time by penetrating and holding all our moments together; commitments create a person.

Peter recognized, like the shepherds and wise men, that we need to find something worthy of our devotion. So when Jesus called him, he followed. By his commitment to Jesus, he was able to start finding himself. He found that his insight into good and evil enabled him to recognize the Christ; nonetheless, he did not know enough and had to be severely rebuked immediately after the moment of recognition. By his commitment he learned that a true master washes his disciples' feet; that is, he serves. Peter thereby learned the lesson Mary knew so well—that receiving our elevation means serving others. He also learned that he was not self-sufficient; for when he tried to stand by his own strength, he failed—he ran when Jesus was arrested and then denied him when questioned. By his commitment to follow he learned that he was loved more than he loved; that he might deviate from his Lord, but his Lord never ceased returning to him.

Had Peter not taken on a commitment, he would not have learned what he was and who he was; without a commitment to one who loved him, he would not have been able to expose all that he was and have it transformed, so that he became a greater, nobler, devoted man who was indeed a rock. Without commitment he would not have known that great transforming love.

Our true selves are being created not only in obvious forward progress; even our deviations help shape us and form us, as they did Peter. We quietly and gradually become stronger as our true selves emerge in following our Lord. We find the spiritual strength to remain loyal in all our commitments to friends and family. We have the opportunity to find joy in other people because we have the strength to stick with them and both to know and be known by them more deeply.

All of us vacillate in our commitments, especially in our commitment to God. Our pilgrimage is not like following a superhighway, where we go straight from where we are to our destination. We zigzag, and at times apparently drift. Sometimes we even seem to have lost our way. I illustrated this in my own case with the problem of self-sufficiency. Each follower's spiritual life is unique: each has had its own distinct, winding course; but I think we have now reached a place where we can receive something that is true of all of us in our pilgrimage.

In our journey, in fact at the very first arch of the gateway, we learned that initially we do not choose to believe in God. We do not at first have any genuine idea of the kind of reality he is, nor are we able to picture his reality. He who is invisible is not imaginable. All we can do is to decide not to give ourselves to anything that is of this world; it is to attend and hold fast to that hole that is at the center of ourselves. Our journey through the various arches of the gateway and the various steps along the way open us up to receiving his Spirit. They have helped to shrink our false self and put us into the right shape to receive him. *But the juncture at which God may come has no law;* it can be at the very first archway. He comes to us secretly and silently, so much so that we ourselves do not know when it was he first entered. He enters and his Spirit grows in us as we continue our journey. When we consciously choose to believe in him, we are only *recognizing* what has already been accomplished. Our recognition, which we may think of as a conscious choice, may indeed feel momentous, a glorious moment, but nonetheless it is but a recognition of his work in us. It is a work made possible because we have been open to receive him by our refusal to be filled by anything else. We choose to *remain* committed to him because of the nourishment we receive, but initially we do not choose.

Even after we have recognized his reality, our awareness of him is not always strong. It expands and contracts in the ways we have described in every stage of the journey. But though we are not always aware of him, our relation to God continues. It is able to withstand enormous abuse and failures on our part. Just as he has come to us without our being aware of who he even is, so he grows within us even when we are unaware of it. Our journey is really the endurance of his continuous growth. His presence creates the continuous pull and tug of all the steps along the way, and in that struggle he shapes us. So we can understand the apostle Paul with utter literalism when he tells us that we can rejoice both in our losses, renunciations, and sufferings, as well as in our joys; for in both the Spirit of God is with us and growing within us without fail. He will accomplish what he has begun; we only endure the joy and turmoil spiritual growth brings to us, while at the same time we face the regular ups and downs of this life.

Our awareness of the reality of God is not a discovery of God, but a recognition of his work that has been taking place all along. The love of God, most manifest on the cross, has been at work within us before we are called upon to believe it and be witnesses to it.

Our renunciations along the journey have opened us to the presence of God's Spirit. But we have not earned or merited his coming. He seeks to give himself to us; we simply, *without realizing it,* allowed an opening for him to enter. He then grows within us. The pull or conflict between what we are and what we are to become is a suffering that, despite the fact that it hurts, enables us to recognize that a new creation is being made. Though we do not yet fully know what we are to be, we recognize we are moving in the right direction.

Part 3

THE CROSS

We have now reached a decisive stage in our journey. The gateway we have entered and the steps we have taken along the way lead us to the foot of the cross. Jesus, who pioneered a way for us to the Father and whose path we are following, ended up on a cross. There he faced his final and most decisive trial. We ourselves are not called upon to endure the cross; only he faced that trial. We are instead called upon to become witnesses of the cross. Our journey has put us into a position that enables us to see and understand what took place there. We have been led to this point in order to receive its blessing and to proclaim it for the sake of others.

Our ability to perceive and receive what happened there is proportionate to our renunciations and our humility. As blindness is the price of pride, sight is the gift of humility. It of course takes intelligence to understand anything, but it takes intelligence illuminated by humility to be a witness to what happened on the cross. Without humility, the cross means little to people. It is just another case of a good man who was brutally killed, and out of that some people have built a theory that his death is our means of salvation. But our journey has been one in which the way we think has been deeply shaped by the development of humility.

The renunciations we made to enter the gateway, and our painful steps along the way, have made us more realistic about ourselves. We know in our very bones how strong and powerful evil is and what an effort it takes to free ourselves from the false world it creates. We can thus be a witness to what Jesus endured on the cross. By our suffering we can understand his; by the evil we have resisted, we can imagine to a degree what it would be to endure the *full* effect of evil. We can imagine his temptation to lose faith in his Father when he was bearing its full weight. We can recognize the greatness of Christ who, unlike us, endured its full force. We can understand why we cannot. We can thus be witnesses to the cross as a victory; for Christ by his refusal to be overwhelmed by evil won a victory over evil. Wholly apart from the resurrection, the cross is itself a triumph, not a defeat. Those who have resisted evil, and walked as far as the cross, can perceive its glory. We can of course only attain some understanding, for what occurred is a mystery. A mystery has many layers that we can increasingly understand but whose fullness we cannot exhaust.

Now, from the vantage point of our pilgrimage so far, let us look once again to that great focus of the Christian faith, the cross of Christ. What we have experienced so far in our pilgrimage will act as a ray of light to illumine for us the great mystery enacted there.

eight

THE VICTORY
OF CHRIST

In our pilgrimage we have learned the meaning of renunciation, dependence, and the mystery of communion; we have become more deeply aware of the destructive effects of might, social position, and self-seeking. These, and other things we have learned, help illumine many of the events of Christ's passion. In fact, they help explain why we refer to the events as a *passion*. Though the meaning is now obsolete, passion once meant the condition of being acted on, especially by outside influences. It is to be passive; to endure the effects of external forces on us. So when the New Testament events are referred to as Christ's passion, it means that Jesus is being acted on. He is not in charge of events. He does not run from them; he willingly exposes himself to them. He recognizes the cross and the events surrounding it as something that he will endure because it is his Father's will.

Besides his Father's will, he is also subject to force. He endures brute compulsion from soldiers as they beat him, march him to Golgotha, and nail him to the wood. He endures not only the pain, but also the humiliation. He is stripped of all social status by being convicted as a criminal. This must have been a terrible humiliation because we find in the New Testament reports of his passion great emphasis on the fact that the two trials were not fair. Not only were the priests at the Sanhedrin trial unable to find witnesses to bear out the charges, but the witnesses they did produce contradicted each other. It is emphasized that at the criminal trial Pilate, the Roman governor, said he found no harm in the man and wanted to release him. Our pilgrimage has increased our consciousness of how important social position is to our own self-respect. So the humiliation of his condemnation by the highest religious authorities of the day and his criminal trial should help us better realize what he endured. He was not just killed, he was publicly stripped of all position and shamed. His shame went very deep—he was mockingly clad by the soldiers in a purple robe, and jeered at by the priests who shouted, as he hung from the cross, "He saved others; he cannot save himself" (Matt. 27:42a). Can you imagine the roar of laughter such a remark raised? The very inscription over his head, "The King of the Jews," suggests the sort of treatment accorded by cruel people to a mentally deranged person, a fool, who thinks he is king. There was no glamour or glory in such a death. It was a very embarrassing way to die.

His passion also included the endurance of evil, the full force of evil. This above all we are asked to see; for in our lives we also suffer the effects of evil. It marks all our relations; it scars our lives; it kills people. Still, none of us ever bears the *full* force of evil; we never experience its *full* effects. We never feel the full consequences of its weight. But Jesus did; he endured it on the cross.

We can grasp, in part, what this means by meditating on a familiar scene that occurs in the passion story. Immediately after the Last Supper, Jesus led his disciples to an olive grove called Gethsemane, and asked them to sit and watch while he prayed. His disciples tell us that Jesus was in terrible agony—agitated and trembling. Even to their sleepy eyes, his distress was evident. At the time they did not know what to make of it. But his prayer gives us some indication: "My Father, if it be possible, let this cup pass from me" (Matt. 26:39b).

I believe that he was beginning to experience that terrible emptiness that led him later on the cross to cry out, "My God, my God, why hast thou forsaken me?" (Matt. 27:46b). People have often tried to soften the shock that these words arouse by pointing out that Jesus was quoting from the beginning of one of the Psalms. He was, but that does not change the fact that he chose these words to quote, that he felt forsaken.

Apparently Jesus normally felt God's presence; he had an openness that allowed God's Spirit to be fully present. He looked always to his heavenly Father, and because he did, the Father was nearly always present to him. But in the garden a dread was upon him—a vacuum began to take over. God's presence was not there as it usually was. Jesus began to sense what lay before him: perhaps God was going to withdraw from him *fully*—he was to be abandoned; the space within him that God occupied would be left void, empty. He was to be at the farthest distance of all from God.

That was the dread that was upon him, so that he sweat great drops like blood. And he prayed that this trial, this cup, this terrible complete absence of God's Spirit, would not happen. Death on the cross was a physical death—a terrible way to die. But that death had to be endured while the presence of God was being withdrawn. In the garden he began to sense that withdrawal: he became aware of the possibility that God would withdraw completely and he would be left alone—left to suffer the complete absence of God while hung on a cross, exposed to the humiliation of penal execution and the mockery of those who hated him. He would descend to hell; for that is what the full absence of God means.

Now perhaps we can understand why he taught us to pray, "Lead us not into temptation" and told his disciples in the garden, "Pray that you may not enter into temptation." People find it offensive to be told that we are to try to avoid temptation. They think we ought to be brave and face temptations, to find ourselves strengthened by the fight and conquest, instead of cowering before dangers and trying to avoid them. We have also seen that there are those temptations that form the gateway that leads to the Father; these temptations we are not to avoid, though they can defeat us. But when Jesus teaches us to pray, "Lead us not into temptation," temptation here means to be exposed to evil that is so deep and so destructive that it can entirely destroy us and consume our soul. It is the evil he faced in the garden of Gethsemane and on the cross. It is the temptation in which the joy of God's presence is utterly gone; it is the feeling of being utterly forsaken. We are to ask our Father not to lead us into that.

On the cross he knew that he was forsaken, but before that in the garden he had already begun to feel it. He prayed that it might not happen. But it did. And when it did he did not understand why. He cried out, "My God, my God, why hast thou forsaken me?"

In the garden we see how hard it was for Jesus, the very image of God, to follow his Father's will. Yet in the garden we find him consenting to God's will: "Let this cup pass from me; nevertheless, not as I will but as thou wilt" (Matt. 26:39b). When the dreaded thing had come to pass his last words on the cross were, "Father, into thy hands I commit my Spirit" (Luke 23:46b). He consented to endure this dreadful death; he gave himself up to it, a death of body and a death more terrible than any bodily death, the death a person knows when forsaken by God. The one who knew no sin, who had always been open to the Father's presence and known him, now was left empty of that Spirit. Yet he loved and longed for the Father. When Job was afflicted in various ways, he was tempted to "curse God and die." Jesus, when he was utterly forsaken, overcame the temptation to "curse God and die."

Later what happened was explained by Paul, as far as it can be explained: "He made him to be sin who knew no sin" (2 Cor. 5:21a). He who was one with the Father, whose heart, mind, and soul loved and longed for God, and who knew the rich, glorious presence of his Father, was put at the greatest distance anyone can be from him. And he endured it. In an agony that no one else had ever experienced, an agony no one else can endure, an agony no one can comprehend. He had not expected to be forsaken. To die, yes; but not to be forsaken. He had had apparently no hint of it until that night in the garden. But as the Scripture puts it, he was obedient unto death. He still looked to the Father, trusted him, loved him, though he had been forsaken and did not know why.

Christ endured the Father's complete absence. This is to endure the effect of evil; for evil destroys communion, and the full effect of evil is to destroy all communion. Evil at bottom is the refusal to recognize the reality of others, to refuse to restrain ourselves, so that another does not have room to live and develop freely. We have not made enough room for each other; our appetite for our own worth and significance has not left enough room for others. Most of the time we do not know each other very well, nor our Father, nor ourselves, because we cannot limit the boundless horizon that is our own overexpanded self and let another person appear independently of our interests. Yet the Father does not allow our evil to have its full effects. He does not allow it to drive him away from us completely. He does not leave us to experience his full absence. He sustains us to an extent, even when we are utterly unaware of him. Only Christ endures the complete absence of the Father; only he bears the full effects of the destroyed communion that results from evil.

Our joy and our hope is that the greatest depths of evil that killed him could not overwhelm him. They did not overwhelm him or overcome him; for he did not "curse God and die." He dies enduring the effects of evil, enduring the greatest distance from God, still longing for that presence. That was the victory over evil; to endure it and not to curse God; to endure it and not know why; to endure it and to trust the Father. We see that evil, for all its power, is not all-powerful, for it could not destroy his love and trust. His goodness is greater than evil; it is able to break his body but not his will. It could not change the direction toward which he looked and to which he was pointed.

Each of the arches of the gate and steps along the way reveals to us the wisdom that comes from suffering. Our desires for goods and what goods stand for can drive us and make us miserable; but such unhappiness can teach us that we do not live by bread alone. We learn from the uncertainties of this life that we must trust that our hunger will be satisfied, without any advance guarantees. In our search for personal worth and status, we suffer from the power of social standards that divide us. We are exposed to the fickle impersonality of chance and force that have no regard for our social position or our moral worth. This can teach us of our essential unity and teach us to be compassionate toward all who suffer. All of these experiences, as well as the way we are shaped by each step along the way, enable us to be witnesses of the suffering of Christ on the cross. The Greek word that is often translated *witness* is equally well translated *martyr*—one who suffers. We can witness his suffering because we have suffered—not just any kind of suffering, but the suffering that comes from following the path he pioneered.

Because we have wrestled with evil and know its power—its destructiveness of community—we are able to participate in the cross. We know in our own bodies and minds and hearts the kind of conflict that took place on the cross between Christ and the full force of evil. The wisdom we have gained from our suffering enables us to enter into the depth of the divine wisdom of the cross. There we see most fully in the death of his Son, in the suffering he endured, that there is no life apart from God. He experienced at the greatest distance from the Father the kind of death that results from the total absence of God. Our struggle with evil—a struggle through which our true life is begging to emerge—is only possible because we are spared the full effects of evil. We are spared being placed at the greatest distance from God. He has not allowed us to experience his complete absence. We can make a pilgrimage because we have been spared an exposure to evil that would completely destroy us. We could not bear what only the Son could bear. We may find life because the Father loves us enough to send his Son; we may find life because his Son loves enough to be able to endure the full effect of his Father's absence.

In the cross we see most fully the wisdom of God. We are to be witnesses to the way God has used his power. He has not used force to bring us back; he has restrained himself; he has renounced the use of might. He has not abandoned us for our failure to turn to him. But he has used his great and unfathomable power to bear the terrible catastrophe of evil by letting it tear his Son from himself. He asks us to see, to perceive that great loving power and that of his Son which painfully endures this rupture. He calls us to see the wisdom of restraint, of what we may find by pulling ourselves back and recognizing the reality of the communion that we may have with him and the life that it brings. We are asked to see and confess that Jesus is the Wisdom of God.

Our opportunity to find our true life has been made possible by Jesus' death. Neither before Jesus' coming nor after it has anyone had to bear the full effects of evil. That was his destiny. His greatness, his glory is that he was able to accept it and endure it.

We do not know our true selves, our true life apart from God. The power of evil over us leads us to seek fullness of life in material goods, and in the prestige social status can bring us. We succumb to the temptations of seeking security, relying thoughtlessly on chance and might to maintain us. We are called to die to such a life, to walk behind Jesus and be free of it. We are thus able to find the true life that comes from communion with his Father.

Communion at its highest is love. Our last step is to love him—to love the Son of the Father, just as the Father loves him—because of his endurance of evil for our sake. The Son whom we love points us to the Father; for Christ achieved his goal as Son, his victory over evil, by a humble trust and love of the Father. His love kept him pointed to the Father and kept a connection with him even though he was at the farthest distance from him and though he could not feel his presence. So too are we steadily freed from the power of evil and healed of its scars, as we love the Son who was sent by the Father, and love the Father who sent his Son for our sakes. It is by love that we are drawn into life, into the true life.

The cross reveals to us the horizon of our true selves. We are at the threshold of the restoration of communion and the community it creates. We are at the place where we are able to respond with love to that love which elevates us into heirs.

nine

THE MYSTERY OF
GOOD AND EVIL

We are now ready to begin a new phase of our pilgrimage. We have entered the gateway and taken the steps that lead to the cross of Christ, of which we are to be witnesses. But the journey we have made has been spoken of as if it were along a flat plane surface. We now need to think of our journey as a spiral staircase, which goes round and round but ascends to a higher level at each turn. Our pilgrimage is like a spiral ascent; for we never cease to re-meet the temptations we have met at an earlier period of life. We never leave them behind us completely. Again and again, perhaps separated by years, we become tempted by material goods and neglect to attend to that hole at the center of ourselves. We lose a friend or a loved one, or experience the horror of a hospital ward, or see at first hand the senseless brutality of war, and our faith in a loving Father is shaken. Each and every temptation, each and every step we have made, returns to challenge us again. They may return assuming a different shape or a new form several times.

This may discourage us at first. But we should be encouraged by the fact that we are mounting a spiral staircase. We are not going round and round in a circle on a flat surface getting nowhere. Instead we are making spiral turns that lead us upward. Each time we re-encounter a particular difficulty we are by this experience better able to understand Christ's struggle and victory on the cross. Our pilgrimage returns us again and again to the cross, increasing our need for forgiveness, enriching our understanding of God's love, and making us better witnesses to what happened there. In this way we participate with increasing fullness in Christ's passion. So there is progress. We become more aware of God's love for us; we become more aware of our true selves.

I

This spiral effect is evident to us if we return to a fact we encountered at the beginning. As we saw there, we often do evil because it appears as something good. Each arch through the gateway consists of a temptation to something we need or that is desirable: bread, security, and recognition of our worth. But now that we have got this far, we learn of a new way that evil can establish its power over us.

Evil becomes more treacherous after we have made some progress in resisting it. It becomes more treacherous after we have learned to recognize some of the ways it disguises itself as something we need or that is desirable. It is after we have made a good start on our pilgrimage and gone several turns of the spiral that we encounter evil at a new level. We can now be betrayed by our own best intentions. For it is precisely because we desire to be rid of evil, heartily desire it, that we become ensnarled. It is precisely because we recognize its destructiveness and its ugliness that whenever we see it, we hate it. But to deplore evil can be a way to fall into *deeper* evil; our hatred of it can drag us deeper into it.

This can happen in several ways. One of the most common is to become hateful. This happens because by becoming a follower of Christ, we have declared our desire to be rid of evil. We may have more or less put our most glaring evils behind us. Precisely because we have encountered it in our pilgrimage and rejected it we become proficient at seeing evil in other people's actions. We see it at every turn; and indeed we are correct, for it is there. But because we hate evil, we do not realize that what we see in others is also in us. We do not admit the evil that in spite of our progress is still within us. So we have no pity or sympathy for others. We roundly condemn what we see without any compassion. We thereby lose communion with them. We become alone. Our very hatred of evil, the evil we still bear and the evil outside us, leads us into greater evil: the isolation of the proud. We can no longer properly perceive, experience, or witness the compassion God displayed on the cross, namely his love for sinners.

Another reaction to the evil that we still bear in our own person is self-hatred. Instead of looking outward and criticizing others, we may despair of our own sinfulness. H. L. Mencken once wrote an editorial entitled "A Good Man Gone Wrong." He tells of a book he had just read by a man condemned to the electric chair. He had murdered his mistress's husband. Throughout the book the author protests that he really was a good man. Mencken agrees. What had gone wrong, Mencken declares, was that the man had been a believing Christian and had desired to be and was a good person. But he had got himself involved with a married woman, and his conscience was compromised. He felt utterly lost in evil. When the woman planned the murder of the husband, her lover was already lost. His "perfection" had already been destroyed by the affair so that nothing mattered any more. He went robot-

like through the business of murder as one already con-
demned to hell for his affair.

We may have a picture of ourselves as good people, and
we can by God's grace indeed be good people. We may
have made considerable progress in our spiritual pilgrimage. That progress can now become the very weight that
pulls us down. For we are not perfect, and we can so easily commit an act that for us destroys the picture we have
built up over a lifetime. Such an act can lead us to self-
hatred. The self that we have seen suddenly revealed is
one we cannot tolerate. This self-hatred can lead to
extreme actions, but even if it doesn't, we are by our own
self-hatred unable to receive and enjoy God's love for us.

Another way we can become victims of the treachery
of evil is to try too hard to be good. Our very love of God,
our very admiration of the goodness of Christ's life, our
very commitment to service and concern for others, can
lead us to try to perform actions that are beyond our spiritual strength. We simply are not good enough to perform
some acts, which others can bring off. Some of us simply
cannot look after an aged parent; some of us cannot care
for an invalid or retarded child. We may try to, and get
along fine for a while. But then in time the burden
becomes too great; the sacrifices irritate us; the affection
and good intentions we started with begin to be replaced
by bitterness, self-pity; and secretly we start to hate.

We are at a very tricky place indeed; for there are burdens that we *should* bear and that are indeed beyond our
strength. These burdens can teach us that our strength is
limited and that we have to ask God, again and again, for
the goodness and strength to bear them. What we need to
avoid is the zeal for doing good that causes us to plunge
into tasks that are not our calling. Some of these are
actions we plunge into precisely because we cannot bear
the guilty feeling we get from inaction. Sometimes we
plunge in because we know that a truly good person would
undertake the task, and we cannot bear the thought that

we are not truly good. Not to act would be a confession that we are less than we would like to think. So we plunge in over our heads. Such a plunge can destroy our faith when we discover we are not richly rewarded by "good feelings" and a sense of achievement. The way of service becomes for us tiresome and disappointing. We become resentful about the load we are bearing.

We need to admit that our pilgrimage is a long one, not a few steps or rungs. We have to learn to be realistic about what is well ahead of us and not try to jump ahead. We are indeed to engage in service, but we have to be able to live with a guilt over imperfections that we cannot remove by attempting to perform noble deeds. To try to leap far beyond where we are can lead to even greater evil.

These then are three ways evil can reestablish itself over us. We betray ourselves more deeply into evil by our inability to accept our own imperfection. But to experience our lack of mastery over evil can give us a greater realization of our dependence on God. It can lead us more fully into his love. We do not have purity, but Christ does. He was not overcome by evil on the cross, but could endure its full power. We are attached to him by a rope like mountain climbers. Again and again we are dragged down over hidden holes and crevices, and often lose our footing altogether. But we are attached to him by the rope of his love for sinners. We can always return to the path by drawing on that love.

II

We can now move to a still higher level by asking about our responsibility for evil. Neither the initial attractiveness of evil and unattractiveness of good, nor the greater treachery of self-satisfaction or self-hate, enables us to escape our responsibility. We see this emphasized in the story of Adam and Eve.

Adam and Eve do not fully understand what God means when he tells them the consequences that would follow if they disobey him by eating of the fruit of the forbidden tree. They are like children. A child does not fully understand the warning, "Don't touch that! It will kill you." The child may realize that there is something fearful to be avoided, but its understanding of death is limited by a lack of experience. Adam and Eve lack experience; they are innocent. This innocence is taken advantage of by the serpent. He is more experienced, or at least pretends to be. "Surely you won't die if you eat of that fruit," he says. How many times have we been led into trouble by someone who seems to be more sophisticated than we are, who claims to know by experience that such and such is really all right? And then too, the apple looks good; wisdom is desirable. "The woman saw that the tree was good for fruit and that it was a delight to the eyes, and that the tree was to be desired to make one wise" (Gen. 3:6a). So the story stresses that there is inexperience, that someone takes advantage of that inexperience, and that what is evil appears very attractive. But all this does not relieve Adam and Eve of responsibility.

The same is true with us. We can plead all that Adam and Eve could plead as excuses, and an additional one as well. We can complain about the bad influences of society. We are raised in a society that is often corrupted by evil, and raised by parents who are not perfect. We become involved in evil by the very process of growing up as social beings. Yet, though this is true, we still cannot account for why we choose to do evil. For even when we overcome some of our ignorance, even after we gain some experience, even when we become mature enough to recognize the deceptive mask worn by evil in the social mores of our time, even then we still sometimes do evil. Why? Why does it have a grip on us? Where does it get that power? Why are we so bound to it that try, try, try as we may, we still, underneath all our claims and good intentions, powerfully desire to be noticed, to be recognized, to be important? Why do we find our desire to be someone remarkable rise up? Why are we so conscious of the way we look in the eyes of others? Why are we so anxious? As Paul lamented in bewilderment, after he had made great progress in his spiritual journey, "I do not understand my own actions. For I do not do what I want, but I do the very thing I hate" (Romans 7:15).

Evil is one of the ways we learn that we ourselves are a mystery; for we are not in full control of ourselves and cannot find any method of gaining control. We do not know why we are so full of desires to be recognized, to receive more recognition than we give. We do not know why we live in the unbounded horizon that is ourselves so that we so easily see everything from our own point of view. Why are we this way and why do we *continue* to be this way? These questions seem to transcend all the answers of philosophy, psychology, and sociology. The mass of surreptitious desires for self-aggrandizement that surface again and again, the failures to be fair to others, are not psychological or social disabilities of a person who is ill. They are hard facts about normal people. They are also moral failures. It is not bad people who lament them, but good people. It is saintly people who complain the most. Saints, because they are so much better than most of us, are more aware of the mystery of their own life that is gripped in evil. They can say, "I do not understand myself."

The mystery of the power of evil over us, the mystery of our own lack of self-mastery, is not a truth that is easily learned. It is also not a truth learned just once or twice. It is learned again and again in our successes and failures, and recognized more and more the better we become. It causes a suffering that indeed brings greater understanding of our dependence on God's love.

In exploring evil at this level—when we have got beyond ignorance, inexperience, deceptiveness, and treachery—we are dealing with evil as original sin. We have reached the place where we are describing a state or condition of bondage. We choose to do evil—that is, we cannot escape responsibility for our actions, despite all mitigating circumstances—and yet we do not seem to be in control of ourselves. This condition is called original sin.

Lack of self-mastery is one way to become aware of the state or condition of original sin. But never in this life do we experience or feel its *full* force. Only Christ does: only he has been the farthest distance from God when he was on the cross. There he experienced the full consequences of sin. None of us is called upon to endure that. We can, however, increase our understanding of original sin, and gain greater understanding of ourselves, by performing an experiment. Try to imagine what it would be like to experience complete isolation. When you do this, you will have a much better idea about the state of original sin and the power of evil over us.

To assist your imagination, I will quote a passage found in an old magazine that describes the experience of complete isolation. It happened in a dream to a pious miser who had steadily closed off his heart from everyone.

One evening, as by my lamp I drew up my accounts and calculated my profits, sleep overpowered me. In this state I saw the Angel of Death come over me like a whirlwind. He struck me before I could plead to be spared his terrible stroke. I was petrified, as I perceived that my destiny throughout eternity was cast, and that to all the good I had done nothing could be added, and from all the evil I had commited, not a thing could be taken away. I was led before the throne of him who dwells in the third heaven. The glory that flamed before me spoke to me thus: "Carazan, your service of God is rejected. You have closed your heart to the love of man, and have clutched your treasures with an iron grip. You have lived only for yourself, and therefore you shall also live the future in eternity alone and removed from all communion with the whole of Creation." At this instant I was swept away by an unseen power, and driven through the shining edifice of Creation. I soon left countless worlds behind me. As I neared the outermost end of nature, I saw the shadows of the boundless void sink down into the abyss before me. A fearful kingdom of eternal silence, loneliness, and darkness! Unutterable horror overtook me at this sight. I gradually lost sight of the last star, and finally the last glimmering ray of light was extinguished in outer darkness! The mortal terrors of despair increased with every moment, just as every moment increased my distance from the last inhabited world. I reflected with unbearable anguish that if ten thousand times a thousand years more should have carried me along beyond the bounds of all the universe I would still always be looking ahead into the infinite abyss of darkness, without help or hope of any return—. In this bewilderment I thrust out my hands with such force toward the objects of reality that I awoke. And now I have been taught to esteem mankind; for in that terrifying solitude I would have preferred even the least of those whom in the pride of my fortune I had turned from my door to all the treasures of Golconda.[1]

Now let us see how this experience of complete isolation relates to original sin. The traditional designation of original sin is pride. Many of us would never think of describing ourselves as proud, especially those of us who lack self-confidence and who suffer from low self-esteem. We feel just the opposite of proud. But "pride," when used as a description of original sin, points primarily to only one thing, namely standing apart from others, standing alone. To have pride is to be alone in your inmost self. It is this aspect of pride that has led to the use of that word to describe original sin.

God can bear to be alone because he is self-sufficient. He has such fullness of life as Father, Son, and Spirit that he does not need anything or anyone else. He can bear to be alone because it is true that there is nothing else on his level. But we cannot endure to be alone, as we saw with the miser. We have not got the resources to live a full life on our own. We need other people to be in communion with, to enter into contact with, and by such exchange to live with joy. We are, in addition, creatures made by him, and therefore always dependent, always in need of him in order to have life. This is why original sin is also often described as the desire to be like God: the desire to be independent, to be able to live without any limits.

In the ancient story of Adam and Eve, we are warned of the dangerous consequences of trying to live like God. A tree is put in the middle of the garden of Eden, and Adam and Eve are told not to eat its fruit, or they will die. The forbidden tree is to remind them that they are limited; that they are creatures; that they live only by obedience to their Lord.

But as we know, the serpent tells the woman, "You will not die. For God knows that when you eat of it your eyes will be opened, and you will be like God, knowing good and evil" (Gen. 3:4–5). The serpent tells a half-truth. By eating of the tree they set aside all limits, and they indeed become like God. But unlike God they cannot sustain such a position. They do not die all at once—again the serpent is half-correct—but they must now live outside the garden. That is, they must now be separated by a distance from God—the source of their life—and live as they have chosen, like God, namely out of their own resources. But unlike him, their resources are not enough. We see humankind in the form of their two sons, Cain and Abel, sinking more and more into conflict and disharmony, until one brother kills the other. Now that they have rejected their limitations in the form of a forbidden tree, people cannot respect the limitations formed by other people. They abuse and outrage each other. They indeed do not die all at once, but they are in a situation that deteriorates steadily. They move closer and closer to the place where communion between people is extinguished, as we see with the story of the tower of Babel. It is the lowest point reached before God calls humankind back into communion by his covenant with Abraham.[2]

We in our pilgrimage have reached the place where we can recognize the soundness of these ancient stories. They exhibit a recognition on the part of their authors of the impossibility of filling that emptiness at the center of ourselves with the things of this world. They show a realization that only God can feed that hunger, and that he is the foundation for a life that seeks fullness. They are a witness to our alienation and the conflict between us when we fail to recognize God as the basis of our common life. They show the destructiveness that results when we search for a full life from the things of this world. By covering several generations these stories also suggest another thing we have found in our pilgrimage, namely, that we do not learn these truths all at once, but progressively over a period of time.

III

Our isolation is not complete. We are sheltered from the miser's experience of complete isolation. We still have some contact with others. But our contact is limited, and we rarely experience the joy of full communion with others. Every day, in our ordinary lives, we experience to some degree the isolation of original sin. In T. S. Eliot's play *The Cocktail Party*, we have an example of sin's presence in the ordinary circumstances of a marriage that is breaking up.

Each of the characters in the play is isolated from the others and enclosed in his or her own fantasy world, as they all try to find a satisfying life. Lavinia, who makes all the decisions for her immature husband, Edward, decides to leave him. He is completely surprised. It breaks in on him, as he puts it, with the land of jolt you get when going down some stairs and incorrectly expect one more step. He had previously thought that he could never get rid of Lavinia—that she would always be in the way of his finding happiness with Celia, his mistress. Now, of her own accord, she is gone. His normal world is suddenly interrupted and he cannot get his bearings.

The event causes a jolt for Celia too; for she finds that her affair with Edward was really a dream. Now that he is free, he is quite uninterested in her. Now that his wife is no longer there, he slowly becomes aware that he wants her back.

The misconceptions continue to be dispelled. Peter is having an affair with Lavinia. She turned to him because she felt unlovable and tried to prove otherwise. She had tried to see their affair as something lovely and deep; and indeed she was able for a time to think of it that way. But Peter was only pretending to care; his real interest was in Celia. He thought he had an almost mystical, holy relationship with her. They used to go to the theater and concerts, sitting apparently in a deep silent rapport of person to person. But Peter feels that somehow the tie between himself and Celia has been broken. Unaware of Edward's affair with Celia, Peter asks Edward to intercede on his behalf. When Edward tries to, another bubble breaks; for Celia responds to Edward's plea on Peter's behalf with the crushing reply, "Peter who?" There had been no deep silent rapport, as Peter had imagined. Celia had felt rather sorry for Peter and allowed him to take her out a few times, but she had grown tired of his conceit and sense of superiority.

Each person had built a picture of the other that suited himself, and by that false picture each was isolated from the other. Such illusions could not continue indefinitely and they begin to fall like dominoes. When Lavinia leaves Edward, each person begins to experience isolation and to recognize the false ways they have tried to escape from it by creating illusory relationships.

Edward and Lavinia find that the remedy for their isolation is to learn how to pay attention to each other in the mundane relationship of marriage. He needs to realize how insecure she is about her acceptability and lovability, and to help with her bad moments. She has to remember what a little boy he really is. They do not do this particularly well. He clumsily compliments her for looking so lovely in her party dress too often and at the wrong times. She lets him know this, but she realizes that he is trying. They are thus able to mitigate some of the effects of isolation.

Celia, on the other hand, is marked for a different vocation. The isolation she begins to experience with the breaking of her dream is one that she cannot understand. She seeks help from a psychiatrist. When he asks her what is wrong she replies, "I should really *like* to think there's something wrong with me—Because, if there isn't, then there's something wrong, with the world itself."[3] If her emptiness is not an illness, she is completely out of her depth. She eventually describes her feeling as a sense of sin—not of scarlet sin, of the affair she has had or anything she has done. It is merely her profound isolation. She experiences it as horrid. She forcefully recognizes that we do not have the resources to be self-sufficient in our isolation. We have an emptiness at the center of our being that can be satisfied *fully* only by communion with God. She eventually becomes a nun.

IV

The extremes of dreariness, boredom, and isolation lead us to an encounter with the mystery of good. The isolation that we at times feel quite severely can be broken by an awareness of something that is beautiful. Iris Murdoch has a scene in her novel *The Bell* in which a young, unhappily married woman, while visiting the National Gallery, has the following experience.

> Dora was always moved by the pictures. Today she was moved, but in a new way. She marvelled, with a kind of gratitude, that they were all still there, and her heart was filled with love for the pictures, their authority, their marvellous generosity, their splendour. It occurred to her that here at last was something real and something perfect....Here was something which her consciousness could not wretchedly devour, and by making it part of her fantasy make it worthless.... The pictures were something real outside herself, which spoke to her kindly and yet in sovereign tones, something superior and good whose presence destroyed the dreary trancelike solipsism of her earlier mood. When the world had seemed to be subjective it had seemed to be without interest or value. But now there was something else in it after all.[4]

Dora is not a bad person. She is instead a thoughtless person who has not yet grown up. Her mother did not give serious attention to her upbringing, so she just drifted into adulthood. She did not care for academic work, so she became an art student despite very limited talent. At first it was fun to be treated as an adult, to wear sandals, and to have some independence. But she soon drifted into a marriage. She was flattered by the attention and pursuit of a successful art historian twelve years her senior. His oppressive attempts to educate her and his jealous love, both of which kept her on lead-strings, drove her into a thoughtless and abortive affair. Her good looks and her adolescent energy and buoyance gave her great resilience. But they could not make up for the dreariness in which she felt trapped. She only became vividly aware of her isolation precisely as its weight was lifted in the presence of some beautiful pictures.

What Dora experienced is the way good overcomes evil. Good can make evil evaporate. In the presence of beautiful pictures she becomes aware of a reality she cannot absorb into herself, and by absorbing, remain alone. She finds a reality that has the power to break her isolation. She encounters a limit, something that is not herself, but that she does not resent. On the contrary, for its independence and sovereignty she feels nothing but gratitude. Beauty is one way in which we encounter good without resentment. It destroys our pride, causes our aloneness to vanish, and yet the destruction of our egocentricity is not painful but joyous. Beauty holds our attention; it attracts and binds us with an authority that we cannot understand. We have no control over it, but we do not resent its authority and we are able momentarily to receive emancipation through it.

But we often do not experience other people and God this way. We frequently resent the way they limit us, frustrate us, and keep us from getting what we want and feel we need. Good is a paradox: from it in its many manifestations we can receive all that Dora experienced. But it can also be experienced as a barrier keeping us from what we want and feel we need.

We see this paradoxical character of good in the forbidden tree in Eden. The forbidden tree was meant to be a helpful reminder to Adam and Eve that they were creatures, in need of communion with God for their life and welfare. It was a kind of fence to keep them from falling into terrible harm. But they soon came to regard it as a senseless, pointless, arbitrary restriction, keeping them from something attractive and desirable. We ourselves have experienced the same paradox. Throughout our pilgrimage we have found that we have to renounce things that are attractive to us in order to find God who alone can give the fullness we desire. His goodness thus initially appears to us as the unattractive demand to give up many attractive and needful things.

Yet there is another side of the paradox. Other people and God—who often frustrate us and keep us from doing what we want—also attract us. When another person pays attention to us, gives us sympathy, and takes us seriously, we often find ourselves elated. We experience the sheer and unrivaled joy of companionship. Our isolation evaporates, as did Dora's, and we know the preciousness of another reality from which we are so often shut off.

We have here reached a most powerful truth: good has power over evil. It can make it vanish. What Dora found true of pictures, we can also find—and find more powerfully and fully—in the goodness of people. We can find it most fully in the person of God when we turn to him and pray. We can experience a presence that lifts our burdens, removes our isolation, and fills us with joy and peace.

We have also reached a place on the spiral of our journey where we can witness a new level of greatness in Christ's endurance of evil on the cross. We have just seen the power of good over evil, the way good can make it vanish. But this power is not complete. Beautiful paintings can be destroyed by accident or vandalism. Good people can be crushed by events. This is true of Jesus too. His body was broken on the cross. But as we saw, he did not lose his faith, trust, or love for the Father. The full force of evil, though it was able to break his body, could not break his allegiance to his Father. Thus evil is limited; it could not break his tie to God. To reach the full extent of evil, to get to the place where its power can reach no further, is to have reached the faithfulness of Christ on the cross.

Evil is encompassed between the love of the Father for the Son and the Son for the Father. It is in God, in the love between the Father and the Son, that we discover the place where evil finds its boundaries. Christ's endurance on the cross enables us to know that there is something over which evil is powerless. Without his faithfulness on the cross, we would not know this.

Because we have found the place where evil's power can reach no further, we glimpse for the first time why God raised Christ from the dead. We can sense something of the force of Peter's claim, "God raised him up, having loosed the pangs of death, because it was not possible for him to be held by it" (Acts 2:24). Death is the opposite of life, and it is from God that we have life. To be totally cut off from God is to die. Evil did not cut Jesus off from God; it did not capture or encompass him. Jesus was innocent of any reason for being cut off from God. He continued right to the end to reach out toward his Father. He trusted him and loved him, in spite of the unwarranted death he was undergoing, and in spite of the inexplicable way the Father's presence was withdrawn from his consciousness. His innocence and his faithfulness in looking to his Father would thus suggest that his death on the cross would not be final. For he was never cut off by evil from the Father; evil had failed to break his faith in the Father. Could the break of contact that came with death, since it was not a result of his lack of devotion to the Father, be permanent? Would death be able to hold him, when he had never relinquished his desire for the Father, from whose presence all life arises?

It is the purity and goodness of Christ's faithfulness that raises these questions to our consciousness. They have a force to the extent that the greatness and the beauty of his devotion permeate our total being. As the purity and goodness of Christ's faithfulness touch us and progressively fill us with awe and adoration, we become more and more open to a new blessing. We reach the place in our journey where the reality of Christ's resurrection from the dead can become a personal reality for us. We reach a place where we can experience with the disciples the joyous truth that death could not hold him. With his resurrection, the goal of our own journey appears on the horizon. From the reality of his resurrection emerges the hope for our own as well.

Notes

1. Quoted by Immanuel Kant in his *Observations on the Feeling of the Beautiful and Sublime*, trans. John T. Goldthwait (Berkeley: University of California Press, 1960), pp. 48–49. Copyright © 1960 by The Regents of the University of California; reprinted by permission of the University of California Press.
2. See Dietrich Bonhoeffer's *Creation and Fall* (New York: The Macmillan Co., 1974).
3. T. S. Eliot, *The Cocktail Party* (New York: Harcourt, Brace and Company, 1950), 132.
4. Iris Murdoch, *The Bell* (New York: Viking Press, 1958), 203–204; Avon paperback (1966), 183.

Part 4

THE
RESURRECTION

Could death hold him? That question was answered for the disciples by his actual resurrection from the dead. They claimed that he appeared to them. They thus became convinced that evil was not only unable to break his devotion, but its power to shatter and destroy his body and take his life was abrogated. His resurrection from the dead dispelled all doubt concerning the propriety of his trust in God as he endured evil on the cross. It showed that his trust was vindicated. His Father indeed does exist and does have the power to reverse the effects of evil on our bodies as well as on our spirits. The kingdom is to come after all, when all tears are wiped away and death itself shall be put to death.

But he appeared to the disciples, not to us. He thus answered for them the question about death's power to hold him. How shall it be answered for us? Are we to rely on the disciples' report? Are we to trust what they said?

ten

BLESSED ARE THOSE WHO HAVE NOT SEEN AND YET BELIEVE

The resurrection of Christ from the dead may seem like a fairy tale to those who lack any personal experience of a genuine search for God. But even for those who are religious, there are moments when it seems too good to be true. It is completely out of keeping with the normal course of events that a person should be raised from the dead. The long history of humankind's belief in some sort of survival of death, and the periodic renewal of interest, as in our own day, of alleged communication with the dead, seem to be more a reflection of human wishful thinking than of fact. So there is good reason to question the disciples' report.

Nowadays we have a procedure for dealing with reports from distant times. We have developed the skill of historical investigation to sift reports from distant times and to make critical judgments concerning their probability. So there is a generally recognized method, it appears, for dealing with our question. Apparently we can use historical methods to find out whether the disciples' claim is true or not.

But actually historical investigation is inappropriate in this particular instance. People have indeed frequently made historical investigations of the reports. Sometimes they have argued that the disciples' reports that Jesus rose from the dead, along with the extraordinary transformation of the early disciples into people of great certainty and energy, make a strong historical case for belief in Christ's resurrection from the dead. The soundness of this and similar historical arguments is much debated, with an extensive literature, pro and con, concerning the verdict of historical study. But regardless of how strong, weak, or inconclusive the historical case, this is an inappropriate way to treat the disciples' reports. For if we have historical proof of the resurrection, then we are not in the situation in which we love a person who was without power. Christ's passion is precisely the passion of one who endures the evils of injustice, might, and humiliation without the intervention of his Father. All that was left to him when he was forsaken was his innocence, purity, and trust in the Father. We are asked to be witnesses to this and to be attracted and devoted to such an endurance in the face of evil. But if by his resurrection we see that there is a power that can turn back all evil, are we following him because he is powerful or because he is good? The resurrection displays his power; the cross his goodness. How can we believe in the resurrection without losing the possibility of loving him because of his goodness? How can we love him regardless of whether he is vindicated or not if we know that he was vindicated by being brought from the dead? We are caught in a dilemma. If historical investigation shows that the evidence is inconclusive or weak, then it seems we should not believe in the resurrection of

Christ. But if it is strong, it seems to deflect us from the cross. Either way, we are in difficulty.

We are caught in this dilemma only because we have made a pilgrimage. When we have realized that we are to be witnesses to the cross, and have seen that the cross involves Christ's faithful endurance of the full force of evil, then we see the inappropriateness of historical proof. We see that we should not take the disciples' reports and try to turn them into historical demonstration. For if we were to succeed, we would lose the very Lord we set out to establish. To look to Jesus because there is proof that he rose from the dead is not to *follow* him. Jesus himself had no proof that he would be vindicated; he did not use his special relationship to God as a magic wand to ward off all danger. We can only follow a Lord who had no guarantees by being without guarantees ourselves.

The dilemma, which arises precisely because of the pilgrimage we have made, can be resolved in precisely the same way. We resolve it by realizing that our faith in the resurrection is part of our pilgrimage. Faith in the resurrection has its place on our walk. The resurrection of Christ is not to be isolated from our pilgrimage. But faith in the resurrection must come to us as part of *our* journey, part of *that* exploration, and not from some extraneous source like historical evidence.

Faith in the resurrection of Christ and in our own resurrection can come to us by relying on the disciples' reports only as *witnesses*. We ought to rely on their witness and not try to turn their reports into a proof. But the witness of the disciples puts a great barrier in our path. The wonderful witness to Christ's glorious vindication becomes a great barrier to the continuation of our journey. We do not want to be gullible. We do not want to be victims of wishful thinking. Evil in the world is too prevalent and deep, and death too real simply to leap to belief in the disciples' reports. The vista their witness opens up is simply so immense, so far beyond where we now are, that we cannot suddenly and genuinely believe that the path we have so far followed goes *that* far. We need more than the mere claim by his disciples that he rose and that we are to follow him.

So we are tempted by the very greatness of the vista and its distance from where we now are to stop our climb. We are tempted to stay in the vicinity we have so far reached, and not take too seriously the great vista the disciples' witness opens up. Or perhaps we are tempted at times to step off the path—to take the disciples' witness as historical proof. After we have got some historical support, we think we can then return to the path we had so far followed with the solid assurance that it leads to eternal life.

But that is to encounter in a new form a temptation we encountered much earlier. We are tempted to have the kind of religion that thinks we can escape the limitations and necessities of life. There is no guarantee that we can escape from accidental and senseless injury and destruction in our daily life by praying to our Father. Jesus showed us that in the second arch of the gateway. If we could take our resurrection as proved, we would have the ultimate guarantee—against all accidents and death. But we have no such guarantee. There is no *proof* of Jesus' resurrection—there is no escape from the need for faith. To think otherwise is to fail to perceive the witness Christ bore in his entire life and above all on the cross. It was a witness of trust and love in spite of subjection to evil. The resurrection should not make us bypass this. To use the disciples' witness to the resurrection as part of a proof does just that. And we are tempted to use their witness in this way because the vista their witness opens up is so great and so beyond where we now are. Because we have trouble moving forward, forward to a goal that stretches our minds to the breaking point, we are tempted to seek some help from that which does not lie on the path. But what we find off the path can never be brought back and used for our forward progress, for it covers up the witness of the cross.

How then can we move forward? How can we move forward with a genuine conviction of the immense vista that Christ's vindication opens for us? We must learn, deeply and sincerely—learn in the same sense of "learn" that each movement in the pilgrimage so far has involved—that the resurrection of Jesus is to be known by those who love him. The disciples who saw the resurrection were the ones who loved Jesus. Christ, according to the Scriptures, did not show himself to anyone else. Only those who mourned his death were comforted by his appearance. Those who so love him are not deflected by knowledge of his vindication; their knowledge of the resurrection does not deflect them from an understanding of the cross, of his goodness, because they are devoted to him *prior* to such knowledge.

However good a proof you construct out of their witness, it will not enable you to love him or to see why he is lovable. If you do not love him and do not hold to him because of his goodness, then alleged proofs of the resurrection put your following Jesus into the category of following whoever has power in this world. Power acknowledged as sovereign, apart from the recognition of his goodness, is not a knowledge of God. *God's* power or providential rule is exhibited by the cross. For in *this* world evil has might, and that which does not belong to the kingdom of evil is often crushed by it. We are to renounce evil, to hate it, and to love good regardless of whether we can avoid evil's crushing force. We are to love him whether we have any guarantees of rewards or not; for this is what we see in Jesus on the cross. He trusts his Father, though his body is broken and though he is abandoned to mockery. It is to believe in One as the ultimate ruler and ultimate power, in spite of the fact that in this world evil can do us in, and in fact does many people in. Such a faith is to be based on a display of Christ's goodness, his power to endure evil, his trust. It is not to be based upon a proof of his power but on recognition of his goodness and trust, even when he had no power.

Those of us who have renounced evil's authority, though we do not know whether it can ever be vanquished, are able to perceive Jesus' greatness. We can see in the cross a refusal to consent to might. If we love him, if we admire his purity and mourn his fate, we become like the disciples who loved him and *waited*. The disciples loved him, even though they did not believe that he was alive any more. They loved him even though they did not know whether he would rise or not. Because they loved him, he showed himself to them.

There was one of the original disciples, however, who did not see him with the others. He refused to believe their claim to having seen him alive again. That disciple, Thomas the Doubter, is closer to us in this respect than the other disciples. He too had a report to respond to, but he wanted proof. We can thus learn from the way Jesus reacted to Thomas' disbelief.

We do not know why Thomas would not believe their reports. It is simply recorded that he said, "Unless I see in his hands the print of the nails, and place my finger in the mark of the nails, and place my hand in his side, I will not believe" (John 20:25b). It is clear that he wanted proof, a very demanding proof. But he also recognized that if it were true that Jesus had risen from the dead this was not just one more truth in the universe to add to all the other truths. Instead it is a truth that demands one's whole life. Thomas apparently realized this; for when Jesus did appear to him, he exclaimed, "My Lord and my God." Nothing less than commitment; nothing less than complete devotion.

Yet despite such a response, Jesus does not praise him. Jesus does not commend him, but instead compares him unfavorably with those who believed the reports. "Have you believed because you have seen me? Blessed are those who have not seen and yet believe" (John 20:29).

Jesus is here not commending gullibility—praising those who will swallow anything that is pious or hopeful, who are ready to believe without a shred of evidence the most astounding tales. Those who are pronounced blessed are precisely those who love him, those who have themselves encountered good and evil, who recognize the power of evil and yet who love the good, and who perceive in him—in what he did and said, and the way he died—one who is admirable and lovable. They are the ones who themselves have learned wisdom from suffering, and who are attracted by his purity.

The resurrection of Jesus is not something with which one begins the religious life; it isn't the starting point of the pilgrimage. When treated as standing at the gateway to becoming religious, the resurrection seems to many to be a mere myth or fable, a sort of cheap escapism from the reality of death, believed in only by immature people or simpletons. When put at the beginning, it is also greeted with a demand for evidence or proof. For how else, when taken in isolation from a long pilgrimage, is it to be given credence?

Although opinions differ on how much evidence there is for the resurrection, it is safe to say that on any reading there is some favorable evidence. It has not been shown to be a fable. But that should not be seized on as a stepping stone. Instead it needs to be realized that the resurrection does not stand at the beginning of the religious life; nor does it stand in isolation from a pilgrimage. Instead at some place on the spiral ascent, *a place that is not the same for everyone*, we find ourselves receiving the testimony of the disciples as credible. Our intellects accept the report because we see it as coming from those whose knowledge of good and evil, whose love of Jesus, is like our own. They become credible witnesses to us because we recognize them as fellow travelers. *But this is not an argument.* This is a *partial explanation* of why we give our assent so readily. Belief in the resurrection is not something we *strain* to do, push our mind to give its assent, sweat over the evidence for it, or boast over how good the evidence for it is. It is something we recognize we *have* assented to, something we *have* received because it establishes itself within us.

The disciples' report becomes a witness, a credible witness to those who love Jesus. Over the years as we walk along the road, we become increasingly aware of the innocence and faithfulness of Christ on the cross. The greatness of his trusting endurance of the full force of evil means more and more to us. Our consciousness is steadily penetrated and filled with the question, Could death hold him? We mourn his death at the hands of evil men. This is all part of our pilgrimage. This pilgrimage so forms and shapes us that we come to realize more and more that we must rely on a witness and not on a proof. And faith in his resurrection and thus in our own comes in its own good time. It comes without any *additional* strain over and above those we have already endured in our pilgrimage. We simply find ourselves one day responding to the disciples' witness with joy. Our minds become filled with its truth.

Our intellect, when illumined by a knowledge of the mystery of good and evil, when it has learned to be humble, is an intellect that can love the one who died on the cross. An intellect that has hungered for what is not of this world and been nourished by the purity of Christ's life and faith in the face of evil finds the resurrection of Christ the completion and consummation of God's wisdom. We have reached a place on our journey such that we can believe that our path leads vastly beyond where we have so far walked.

The resurrection is not a discovery of reason, any more than the incarnation and cross. But all these impose themselves on the intellect that knows good and evil, that knows what it is to hunger and thirst for righteousness, that knows the food we receive when we turn to Jesus. But again this is not an argument, but a partial explanation. It describes how we receive the disciples' witness, how we give credence to it. An intellect that is formed by a pilgrimage is the mind of a person who is blessed; for it is a mind so illumined by love of him that, at some juncture in its journey, it responds with belief in the reports of the disciples. It is an intellect that finds itself trusting in the vindication of God.

Indeed blessed are those who unlike Thomas do not demand a proof. For unlike Thomas, all those who do not believe are not given a proof. So if they wait for a proof, there may well be none forthcoming. The blessed depend on a report, depend on a testimony. If such testimony is treated as fodder for making a historical argument or proof, then one is deflected from the cross, from the need to renounce evil by making a pilgrimage, and thereby learning what occurs on the cross. Instead, such testimony is meant to bring joy and conviction to that intellect which, because it has made a journey, can receive gladly the reports of those who loved him. We can receive gladly the report that God vindicated Jesus' faithfulness and that Jesus did succeed in pioneering a path to the Father, a path we are to follow all the way.

Our belief in Christ's resurrection and hence in our own may be steady and unswerving. It is more likely to be a conviction that swells up at times, and then dies down, and may even seem to leave us altogether for a while. This is to be expected, for we are still on the road and have not reached our destination. The goal opened up for us by Christ's resurrection is not even very clear or distinct. So much of our life is unredeemed that we have trouble even imagining what it would be like to be completely transformed. This should not be too surprising. Have you not noticed how much trouble writers of fiction have when they try to imagine "heaven," and how biblical writers have to resort to metaphors when they describe the kingdom of God, or the life that is to come? What is to come and what we are to be are only very partially known in the changes taking place in us as we make our pilgrimage. The transformation that is promised is so complete that we are stretched again and again to the point of incredulity. So our wavering should not trouble us too much. We have trouble taking the greatness of God's gift into our limited being. But all things come to those who wait, who do not strain to be far beyond where they now are. We are to take one step at a time: faithfully to resist evil, to love that which is good. We thereby become better and better witnesses to the cross and also grow in our love for the one who came and for the one who sent him. Our Father will see to it that we arrive at the place where we are supposed to be. We will get there even if we waver in our conviction about a goal that is so distant our minds and hearts cannot hold onto it all the time.